· · · ·
PRAISE FOR
Water Magic

Water Magic is an excellent introduction to working with that element. It's also an excellent reference book for experienced practitioners, covering everything from deities to plants, mythology, and sacred sites associated with water. Her bath and wash recipes will go into my recipe book. Highly recommended!

—Deborah J. Martin, author of
A Green Witch's Cupboard

Lilith Dorsey makes the magical element of water come alive in this enchanting book. *Water Magic* delves deep to reveal the mysteries of this elusive element with powerful insights about its history and correspondences. Expect to be inspired by the vast array of practices in these pages, including the many uses of charged water, sacred baths, dream interpretation, magical floor washes, and so much more. I highly recommend this book to anyone who seeks a closer relationship with the element of water.

—Astrea Taylor, author of
Intuitive Witchcraft

This fantastic deep-dive into elemental magic is a brilliant addition to Lilith Dorsey's already stellar bibliography! *Water Magic* will bring you down to the mysterious depths of history and magic and carry you safely ashore to honor this natural force in your own life through plants, crystals, shells, and sacred waters. Filled with stories from around the world, Lilith paints a beautifully diverse picture of the magic of water that will open you up to people and places you've only imagined!

—Paige Vanderbeck, host of
The Fat Feminist Witch Podcast and
author of *Green Witchcraft*

Poetic and beautiful, lyrical and evocative, this book makes an element we encounter many times a day seem as new and fascinating as the first drop of dew on a rose petal…*Water Magic* is a delightful compendium of what must surely be every consideration of the mythology, magick, and majesty of the element of water. Don't let the size fool you. From recipes and rituals to lore and magical attributes, this little book is a powerhouse of knowledge about the sacred and vital element of water.

—Katrina Rasbold, author of
Crossroads of Conjure, Energy Magic,
and *The Sacred Art of Brujeria*

Tremendous! If you are a magickal practitioner looking to deepen your connection to water, this is the book for you. It's also a thorough exploration of water's magickal uses in a variety of traditions, and it doubles as a handy reference guide for working water magick…I really loved this book…Lilith explores a variety of traditions and practices and, in the process, creates the ultimate book on water magick.

—Jason Mankey, author of
Witch's Wheel of the Year

WATER MAGIC

Lilith Dorsey (New York, NY) comes from a Celtic, Afro-Caribbean, and Native American spirituality. She is the editor and publisher of *Oshun-African Magickal Quarterly*, filmmaker of the documentary *Bodies of Water: Voodoo Identity and Tranceformation*, co-host of the YouTube show *Witchcraft & Voodoo*, and author of *Voodoo and Afro-Caribbean Paganism* (Citadel, 2005) and *Orishas, Goddesses, and Voodoo Queens* (Weiser, 2020).

LILITH DORSEY

WATER MAGIC

ELEMENTS
OF
WITCHCRAFT

FIRST EDITION
Fifth Printing, 2023

Book design by Rebecca Zins
Cover design by Shannon McKuhen

Llewellyn is a registered trademark of Llewellyn Worldwide Ltd.

Library of Congress Cataloging-In-Publication Data
Names: Dorsey, Lilith, author.
Title: Water magic / Lilith Dorsey.
Description: First edition. | Woodbury, MN : Llewellyn Publications, [2020]
| Series: Elements of witchcraft | Includes bibliographical references and index. | Summary: "This book explores the element of water and its cultural, magical, and mythological associations, sacred sites, and deities, as well as how to use water in magic, rituals, and spells"—Provided by publisher.
Identifiers: LCCN 2020023284 (print) | LCCN 2020023285 (ebook) | ISBN 9780738764429 (paperback) | ISBN 9780738764856 (ebook)
Subjects: LCSH: Witchcraft. | Magic. | Water—Miscellanea.
Classification: LCC BF1572.W38 D67 2020 (print) | LCC BF1572.W38 (ebook)
| DDC 133.4/3—dc23
LC record available at https://lccn.loc.gov/2020023284
LC ebook record available at https://lccn.loc.gov/2020023285

Llewellyn Worldwide Ltd. does not participate in, endorse, or have any authority or responsibility concerning private business transactions between our authors and the public.

All mail addressed to the author is forwarded but the publisher cannot, unless specifically instructed by the author, give out an address or phone number.

Any internet references contained in this work are current at publication time, but the publisher cannot guarantee that a specific location will continue to be maintained. Please refer to the publisher's website for links to authors' websites and other sources.

Llewellyn Publications
A Division of Llewellyn Worldwide Ltd.
2143 Wooddale Drive
Woodbury, MN 55125-2989

www.llewellyn.com
Printed in the United States of America

CONTENTS

CONTENTS

Part 2:
Working with the Element of Water

Part 3:
Recipes, Rituals & Spellcraft

NOTE

The author and the publisher are not responsible for the use or misuse of the plants and botanicals listed in this book, especially those labeled as toxic or poisonous. Even touching some of these plants can cause a negative reaction. The botanicals and plants listed here are included with their warnings in order to give a comprehensive study of these items.

All plants and botanicals, just like traditional medicines, may be dangerous when used improperly or excessively over time. Be sure to understand completely what you are working with, use only fresh herbs from a trusted and sustainable source, and be aware that strengths may vary.

The author and the publisher do not endorse or guarantee the curative effects of any of the subjects presented in this work.

FOREWORD

For centuries and through many esoteric practices, the elements have been the cornerstones of magical work. Whether it's astrology or modern Witchcraft, these four basic elements create the boundaries and the structures within larger multidimensional spiritual frameworks. They can bring concepts home and make them more readily understandable.

Earth is the ground we walk on, quite literally. It is the rocks, the mud, the mountains. Earth is also our body and the physical manifestation in this life. It is our center and our stability.

Fire is the flame in the hearth. It is the candle, the bonfire, the sun. Fire both warms and destroys. It has the power to transform and incite. Its flame is our passion and our will to go on.

Water is the rain from the skies. It is the world's oceans and lakes, the comforting bath, the morning dew. Water is our blood and sweat, as well as our memories. It rules our emotions and manifests as tears.

Air is all around us. It is our breath, the sounds we hear, and the wind that touches our faces. Air carries seeds and pollen, scents that warn and delight, and songs of culture. Air is our voice, our thoughts, and our ideas.

While every esoteric system applies these basic concepts differently, the elements are there, helping to structure practice and develop a greater understanding of self. For modern witches, the elements are often represented in their magical tools; for example, the chalice might be water and the pentacle earth. For Wiccans more specifically, the elements help raise the magical circle and empower the protective quarters. In tarot the elements flow through the symbolic imagery of the pip cards, and in astrology each element is represented by three signs. For others, the elements provide spiritual guidance for daily meditations, visualizations, spellwork, or life lessons. One might ask, "What element do I need to get through today?"

The following book is the first in a special series that dives deeply into the symbolism and magical use of the elements. Each book focuses on one element and covers everything associated with that element, from spiritual places and deities to practical spells and rituals. For the witch who wants to envelop themselves in elemental practice or for someone who needs a resource on each element, this book and its sisters will provide everything you need.

Written by four different authors from around the globe, each book in the Elements of Witchcraft series shows just how wide and deep the esoteric understanding of the elements goes and how to make that concept work for your own magical and spiritual needs.

Join us on a deep exploration of the magical use of the four elements.

—*Heather Greene*
ACQUISITIONS EDITOR

Introduction

SACRED WATER

Water makes up most of our planet and also most of our bodies. Refreshing, cleansing, strong, and sublime, the power of water is all around us. Humans need water; we could never survive without it. People can live without love, as delightful as it is, but not water. This is especially true when examining the role of water in a sacred context.

Both literally and figuratively, humans are born in water. Floating joyously in our amniotic sacs, our origins are a dark bliss. Then life begins in a flood of possibility, each individual navigating their own unique channels. Each manifestation of water can reveal its own magic and mystery. There are sacred wells that have been used to bless and heal for centuries. Oceans deep and intense. Rivers that allow passage and transformation. Rainwater, waterfalls, storms, glaciers made of ancient ice—all have their own special energy and power.

This book will help us discover all the ways one can celebrate and utilize these sacred waters. It will examine the divine magic of water throughout history—and, more importantly, herstory—and even some of their stories.

The inimitable power of water is both so close and yet so far. When I first began writing this book, I was a bit puzzled as to the reasons the universe had for steering me in this watery direction. I have been a lot of things—a New Orleans Voodoo priestess, a scholar, a filmmaker, an Orisha devotee, and even at times a love witch—but few have ever considered me a water witch. I don't have that many water elements in my astrology chart, and honestly, I'm not even that fond of swimming. Upon reflection, however, more was revealed. Much of the religion of New Orleans Voodoo revolves around the sacred ashe, or energy, of the Mississippi River. Many a time I have stood on her banks offering songs, dances, prayers, and gifts to honor her powerful magic. The connection between the spirits of New Orleans and the water was the subject of my documentary *Bodies of Water: Voodoo Identity and Tranceformation,* which I created shortly before the advent of Hurricane Katrina in 2005.

Another way in which I feel deeply connected to the energy of water is as a devotee of the orisha Oshún. In African traditional religions, Oshún represents the ashe of the river. She is seen as an orisha of love, marriage, money, beauty, dance, and much more. African traditional religions often see special significance where others would only see coincidence. These magical moments surrounding the water have been plentiful in my life. I remember the first St. John's Eve celebration I attended in New Orleans many years ago. I had woken up early, which I often do, and I felt the need to leave offerings at the Mississippi River for Oshún. I quickly hurried to the nearest open market to purchase oranges and honey to leave for her. I walked to the river steps and proceeded to leave my items, tasting the honey and placing the oranges on the edge of the water. As I began to sing and pray, I was joined by two other practitioners, a La Regla Lucumi (Santeria) priest and a woman devoted to the religion. I had never seen them before, and I felt truly kissed by Oshún as I saw them begin to leave offerings and receive blessings from the water. Later that day I attended the St. John's Eve celebration at the Voodoo Spiritual Temple. What followed was a beautiful ceremony for the community and the beginnings of a life that I am honored to still be living today.

Water can help to uncover things, and while some of those things are delightful, others remind you why they were hidden in the first place. I remember another time in the distant past when I had gone to leave offerings for Oshún at the river. This time I was visiting a friend in Virginia who happens to be a Babalawo, an Ifá priest. He brought me to his local river, the James River, to leave offerings and commune with the ashe of Oshún. I went with tears in my eyes and a heavy heart as I pondered my troubles in my romantic relationship of the time. As I waded into the water and bent down to leave my offerings, what did I find at my feet but a dead fish. It was clear the powers that be had answered before I even asked. There have been many other significant times in my life when water has answered my prayers, whether I liked what the actual answer was or not.

Water is associated on every level with the emotions, and oftentimes these can be difficult to deal with. They can be as fierce and intense as a raging thunderstorm or as placid and gentle as a still pond. Getting in touch with one's true emotions and feelings can be really tricky, but the magic of water can help us do this as calmly and effectively as possible.

INTRODUCTION

When I began this book, it felt a bit like approaching water itself. The power and magic of water are formidable topics. Honestly, I looked out across the places, beasts, and beauty that is water and felt that the journey ahead was a bit daunting. There were times when writing it seemed like an existential conundrum, trying to define the scope of water. An element that is ever changing, where no one truly knows its depth, water is a slippery thing to classify. There were many long and sleepless nights, but as my research and resolve began to flow like the waterfalls and the rivers that grace these pages, it got much smoother.

It is my sincere hope that within these pages you find everything a book on water magic should be and needs to be. May the sublime clarity of water guide you on your path!

PART
1

HISTORY,
FOLKLORE & MYTH

Chapter 1

WATER THROUGHOUT TIME AND CULTURE

Humans cannot survive very long without a source of fresh water. Since the start of civilization, individuals have settled near water to help them survive and thrive. Many of these sites have grown into major cities that are still large population centers today. Damascus is arguably the oldest continually inhabited city in the world. It is clear that water determined the site and character of the place.[1]

When we look to early myths and creation stories, there is a clear commonality—namely, that all things are created from water. What follows are tales and magical usages from many different traditions and religions to illustrate how important water is to life itself.

---

1   Nasser O. Rabbat, "Damascus," Encyclopedia Brittanica, last modified November 28, 2019, https://www.britannica.com/place/Damascus.

Ancient Sumerians

In ancient Sumeria there is a myth dating back to approximately 3,000 BCE that tells of the goddess Nammu, embodying the primal oceans, who gives birth to earth and heaven. The Enuma Elish is the creation myth of ancient Mesopotamia that tells of the birth of the gods and goddesses and earth itself. While its exact date is unknown, scholars place the text around the ninth century BCE or earlier.[2] It tells of the beginnings of the world, where all there was on earth was a swirl of water. This water consisted of fresh water, represented as the god Apsu, and bitter, salty water, represented by the goddess Tiamat. They separate and then come back together to create both land and life.

Muslims

In the Islamic tradition water is seen as the source and origin of all life on earth. The Quran talks of blessed water raining down to fertilize and sustain crops, and even how water is seen as a symbol of Allah's power and majesty.

Hindus

The Hindu creation hymn featured in the Rig Veda mentions that in the beginning all was water. Water is both blessing and cleansing in the tradition.[3]

Indigenous Americans

There are also many indigenous American legends that situate the beginnings of the world in and around water.

---

2   King, *Enuma Elish*, LXXII.
3   Webster, Cowell, and Wilson, *Rig-Veda-Sanhitá*, 44.

Iroquois People

The Iroquois people are comprised of six tribes that have inhabited the land for over 4,000 years in western New York and Ontario in North America. The creation story of the Iroquois begins with humans living way up high in the sky, for at this time land did not exist. It came to pass that the daughter of one of the chiefs fell ill. They had no idea how to cure her until one day they received advice from an elder in the community. The elder told them that they needed to dig up the roots of a particular sacred tree to find a solution. The people dug together until they had made a big hole. However, right after they had done this, both the tree and the chief's daughter fell into the hole and down into the space below.

In that space was a giant sea inhabited by two swans. As the girl and the tree hit the water, a loud clap of thunder sounded out. Curious, the swans swam over to investigate. They tried to rescue the girl, but they did not know how. They turned to the great turtle to find out what to do. The turtle, the wisest of all things, explained that these gifts falling from the sky were a good sign. He explained to all who could listen that they needed to find the tree, its roots, and the dirt that was attached. Turtle told them that with this dirt they could make an island for the chief's daughter to live on. The creatures of the world began looking, and the only one who was successful was the toad. The toad searched the depths of the ocean until she finally found the tree. She swallowed a mouthful of the soil and returned to the surface. When she got there, she spit out the dirt and then proceeded to die. The soil then began to spread, for it was magical. Soon there was a giant piece of earth for the girl to inhabit.

Unfortunately, everything in this land was very dark. The great turtle had a solution for this, too. He asked all the digging animals —the gophers, the squirrels, and the rest—to begin digging holes in the sky to let down the light. The chief's daughter went on to become the mother of all things in this new land. Some say she became pregnant when she fell down from the sky into the waters.

Quechan People

The Quechan people, also called Yuma, are an indigenous North American people who inhabit the Colorado River Valley. The creation tale of the Quechan people begins in darkness and water, for in the beginning, that was all there was. The water was rough, and it created a foam that reached up and created the sky. Out of the water emerged the Creator, twin spirits named Bakotahl and Kokomaht. Bakotahl was said to be evil, and Kokomaht was known to be good. During the journey to the surface, Kokomaht had kept his eyes shut. As Bakotahl was rising up from the water, he yelled out to his twin, trying to discover if he had kept his eyes open or shut during the trip to the surface. Kokomaht knew that his twin was evil, so he replied that he had kept his eyes open. The other twin took this advice, but keeping his eyes open upon emerging left him blind. Bakotahl's name translates to mean "the blind one."[4]

Then the twins set about making the sacred directions. Kokomaht took four steps out on the water in each direction and created north, south, east, and west. Next, Bakotahl wanted his turn at creating and started to make human beings. He began to create people out of clay, but they were seriously challenged,

4   Bierlein, *Parallel Myths*, ebook location 1134.

lacking any feet or fingers. Kokomaht laughed at these creations and decided he would do the job himself. He soon made a perfectly complete man and woman. This angered his twin, who sent storms. Kokomaht was angry, too, and stomped his feet. Depending on which version of the story one adheres to, the stomping caused the earth to shake, either sending Bakotahl's creations into the ocean, where they turned into waterfowl, or simply put an end to the storms. In any case, the storms left behind sickness and disease. Kokomaht's humans soon began to multiply and fill the land, making all the tribes of the world. Within the new world there was a frog. The frog became jealous and hateful towards Kokomaht and soon plotted his demise. The frog dug the ground out from beneath Kokomaht's feet, and as he sank, the frog stole his breath. Kokomaht died, his final act teaching people about the transformation of death.

Navaho People

The Navaho are one of the largest groups of indigenous people in North America. They have traditionally inhabited the land in the Southwestern United States. According to the Navaho people, the world humans inhabit today is called the fifth world. The first world contained only a man, a woman, and coyote. This world was quite dark and very tiny, so they quickly climbed into the second, where there was light from both the sun and the moon. It is said that in this world the sun tried to mate with the first woman. She refused, and coyote suggested they travel up to the third world, which was said to be beautiful and wondrous. When they arrived in that world, they were met by the mountain people. They warned them about the great water serpent (in some stories it is an otter) Tieholtsodi. Warning coyote about something was a sure way to get him to do it, for that is his nature. Coyote went and stole the children of Tieholtsodi. Tieholtsodi was furious and sent great floods across the land. The water in the east was black, the water in the south was blue, the water in the west was yellow, and the water in the north was white. All of these many-colored waters began to rise.

The people came to the first man and first woman and asked them what they should do about these floods. They responded by trying to grow mountains and planting reeds to climb up onto in the hopes of escaping the water. The man, woman, and all the other people and animals climbed up into the reeds until they grew so high that they reached the fourth world. The first to arrive in the fourth world was the locust. When he arrived he saw four birds colored black, blue, yellow, and white. They asked locust what he was doing there. They posed several tests so that if locust passed them, they would allow him to stay. The last was an axe-swinging contest during which they hit the locust in the face and flew away. The water began to recede except for that which was located in the south. The first man and the first woman were left to inhabit a small island. They reproduced, and soon there were many men and women.

However, coyote still had the children of Tieholtsodi with him, and because of that the flood waters now continued to rise up, flooding this fourth world. Again they piled up the mountains and planted reeds; this time the beaver climbed up to survey the fifth world. He said it was wet, and the people followed, again taking up residence on a small island in the middle of a huge sea. They begged coyote to return the children of Tieholtsodi, and he did. Now they could all begin their life in this fifth world. The first thing they did was set about removing the excess water; it is said they called on the dark spirit to drain these waters, and their pleas were answered. The water was drained, and in the process the Colorado River was formed.[5]

Cree-Nachez People

The Cree people are one of the largest indigenous tribes in North America. Their land included an area from east of Hudson and James Bays to as far west as Alberta and Great Slave Lake in Canada.

There are many myths about great floods. This one comes from the Cree people. A man heard that a great flood was to come, so he began to build a raft. He started just as the waters were rising. He quickly climbed on board the raft with his dog. The waters lifted the raft high up into the trees. It was then that the dog told his master he must throw him overboard if he wanted to survive. The man loved his dog and did not want to do this, but the dog pleaded that it was the only way and said again that his master must throw him into the water and then remain on the raft for seven days until the water was gone. As difficult as it was, the man threw the dog overboard.

After seven days the water began to disappear. Just as it was almost gone, the man saw dozens of wet people looking for help. As he got closer to them, he saw that they were the spirits of the dead who had perished in the water.

---

5   Bierlein, *Parallel Myths*, ebook location 1891.

West Africans

For creation tales that come from Benin, Nigeria, and other parts of West Africa, it is relatively clear that according to most of the world, the earth and its inhabitants began in water.

In the Yoruba tradition of Nigeria, there are many different variations of sacred tales and stories. In part this is because for over a thousand years it has been an oral tradition where knowledge is passed down from teacher to student or from parent to child. The same holds true for their creation tales. The following is one version of the Yoruba origin story describing the start of the world.

At the beginning the earth was formless and watery. It was neither sea nor land. A supreme being named Olorun lived above all this in the sky. Olorun asked the orisha Nla to help with the creation of the earth. Nla began with a snail shell filled with dirt, a hen, and a pigeon. Nla placed the dirt in a small patch and the birds began to scratch until the land and sea were formed. Chameleon inspected the job and reported back to Olorun that Nla was progressing well. The first place made was called Ilé Ifé.[6]

Haitians

This story comes from the ancient religion of Haitian Vodou, which has become quite popular in recent years. In Haitian Vodou the creator serpent Damballa Wedo and his wife, Ayida Wedo, are deeply connected to water. In their most well-known story, the ancient spiritual teachings from Africa are brought to the Americas. Damballa Wedo is said to have traveled beneath the oceans with the knowledge, while Ayida Wedo slid across the rainbow.

---

6 Bierlein, *Parallel Myths*, ebook location 893.

They met on the other side, intermingled, and spread the sacred knowledge throughout the land.

Japanese

The following is based on the Kojiki, the "Records of Ancient Matters," written in approximately 712 CE. In the beginning there was a great sea of chaos, with all of the elements mixed together. The three divine beings called kami decided to create a world. To start they created many gods and goddesses; two of these were named Izanami and Izanagi. Izanagi was given a magic spear to help create the world. He dipped the spear into the chaos and began to stir it up. When he pulled it out, it was dripping. Some of these drops fell and became an island.

Soon after Izanagi and Izanami came together and began to birth things into the world. They created islands, the first being Foam Island. Then they created the islands of Japan, mountains, waterfalls, and many other things.

Izanami, whose name means "she who invites," next gave birth to a fiery spirit that unfortunately burned her and made her very sick. During her illness she was vomiting, and her vomit transformed into the deity Metal Mountain Prince. She was also sick with other things coming out of her body: her feces turned into mud and her urine became the fresh water. However, her health continued to get worse and worse. Eventually she sunk into the Land of Night. Izanagi followed her and begged her to return. She told him she could not leave as she had eaten the food there and was trapped. When Izanagi finally saw her, he realized she had started to decay. Terrified, he ran away. As he was running, he threw away the combs that had been in his hair. The combs turned into grapes and bamboo as they hit the ground. The night spirit who had been chasing him stopped to eat these things, and Izanagi escaped.

Izanami loved him so and still wished for him to return. She sent eight thunder spirits along with the warriors of the Land of Night in the hope of retrieving him. However, he outran them, stopping briefly to take rest in a peach orchard. When his tormentors approached, he threw peaches at them (peaches are said to drive away evil and negativity). They left quickly, but Izanami persisted. She sent word to Izanagi that if he did not come back, she would kill a thousand people a day. His response was that if that was the case, he would birth a thousand babies a day. This is said to explain why people are born and why they die. Izanagi then sealed up Izanami in the Land of the Night, where she still remains.

After this ordeal Izanagi was said to have refreshed himself by bathing in the water. When he rinsed off his left eye, Amaterasu Omikami, the sun goddess, was born. When he washed his right eye, Tsukiyomi-no-Mikoto, the moon, was born. Lastly, when he rinsed out his nose, Susano-O, the god of storms, was born.[7]

Jewish People

The following is a truncated version of the creation story that comes from the Talmud. God had decided to create a world. The first word that came from his mouth was *baruch*, which means "blessed." On day one he made the heavens and the earth, light and dark, and day and night. God threw a rock into the void and it became the earth. On day two he created the angels. On day three

---

7   De Veer, "Myth Sequences from the 'Kojiki.'"

he made the plants and trees, and he made iron with which to forge tools to cut and manage these plants. He also created Eden, a paradise for Adam and Eve. On the fourth day he made the sun, the moon, and the stars. On day five he made the creatures of the sea, including the leviathan, and those of the air. On the sixth day he made the beasts of the land and also human beings. A number of the angels were upset that God would make other beings and became jealous. God pointed at these angels and they were engulfed in flames.

God then sent the angel Gabriel to obtain soil from the corners of the earth from which to form his humans. Gabriel soon began to doubt his task, for the earth let him know that eventually humans would be the destruction of the beauty that God had created, so God gathered up some dirt and clay himself and molded the first man, Adam. As God prepared to give his new life a soul, the angels, led by Samael (Satan), again began to voice their complaints. God cast them out of heaven, sending them to hell. God then breathed life into his new creation.

It is said that Adam saw the males and females of the other species and asked God to make him a companion. God then created Lilith out of the dust. When Adam tried to make love to her, she refused to lie beneath him. She told him they were both made of dust and she would not submit in this way. In her anger she spoke the unspeakable name of God and then vanished. It is said she went to live among the demons. God then fashioned another woman for Adam, named Eve.

Christians

The Christian creation stories also place a strong dependence on water. Arguably the most famous is the story of Noah and the flood. Flood stories can be found in the mythology of Mesopotamia, Egypt, Greece, Syria, Europe, India, East Asia, New Guinea, Central America, North America, Melanesia, Micronesia, Australia, and South America.[8] The King James Version of the Bible says that God brought

> a flood of waters upon the earth, to destroy all flesh, wherein is the breath of life from under heaven, and everything that is in the earth shall die...And the raine was upon the earth, fortie dayes, and fortie nights.[9]

Despite this watery destruction, the tale is also one of hope. Noah is allowed to build an ark and fill it with two of each animal to ensure the continuation of both humans and animals on the earth.

The concept of sacred waters is as old as time. Early societies clearly saw the vital importance of water as a reason to treat it as a manifestation of the divine. Over time this water began to be seen specifically as a Christian blessing. To start with, Christianity established shrines and sacred spaces around springs and other bodies of water that already carried a mystical significance. As early as the fourth century CE there are reports of clergy pouring blessed water on the insane and commanding the removal of evil from the individual.

Traditionally, when one thinks of holy water, it is water that has been blessed and consecrated by a Catholic priest. However, the efficacy of holy water isn't just confined to the Christian

---

8   Finkel, *The Ark Before the Flood*, 84.
9   The Holy Bible (King James Version), Genesis 6–7.

church. Many may wonder how or why a Catholic mainstay like holy water found its way into traditional Hoodoo and Witchcraft. Well, magic is resourceful; its practices have survived and thrived despite years of prejudice and oppression. Most spells exist today because of their power. Simply put, why would anyone keep doing a spell if it wasn't successful?

Christians use holy water for baptism, a rite which inducts devotees into the faith. It hearkens back to Jesus's own baptism into the religion by John the Baptist in the Jordan River. Over time holy water began to be used not only on people but on places as well. Pope Gregory I in 601 CE advised converting sacred pagan sites such as wells this way, recommending "[pouring] holy water upon said temples...that they might be converted from the worship of demons to the worship of the true God." Over a hundred temples were said to have been transformed in this way. This soon gave way to people using holy water to purify their homes, animals, cars, boats, etc., in a practice that is still carried out today. The Maryknoll Office for Global Concerns, a Catholic organization, has several outreach programs to work for water justice and equality, and states on its website that "water is its own reality, a dimension of planet Earth, ancient and life-giving. It claims its own 'right to be' by the very fact that it is!" They then go on to state that water is a common good and "public water management is accountable to the people and where the common good of the entire community, human and other-than-human, is served."[10]

---

10   "Water and the Community of Life," Maryknoll Office for Global Concerns, first accessed September 1, 2019, https://maryknollogc.org/statements/water-and-community-life.

CHAPTER 1

Scientific Theory

It is no wonder that many of the world's cultures place the origins of life as directly connected to water. Many scientific theories also situate the origins of life on earth in the water. These theories point to hot springs and tide pools as possible locations for the beginning of life as it is known on earth. One specific hypothesis is that life began near a deep-sea hydrothermal vent, with chemical reactions and early life forms thriving there.[11] This occurred approximately 600 million years ago, with actual life forms moving from the ocean to the land roughly 500 million years ago.[12]

The great thinker Leonardo da Vinci was known to be fascinated with water. He believed water to be the true "vehicle of nature," the blood of the world. In this fascinating substance he also observed its paradoxical nature, writing that

> water is sometimes sharp and sometimes strong, sometimes acid and sometimes bitter, sometimes sweet and sometimes thick or thin, sometimes it is seen bringing hurt or pestilence, sometime health-giving, sometimes poisonous. It suffers change into as many natures as are the different places through which it passes. And as the mirror changes with the color of its subject, so it alters with the nature of the place, becoming noisome, laxative, astringent, sulfurous, salty, incarnadined, mournful, raging, angry, red, yellow, green, black, blue, greasy, fat or slim. Sometimes it starts a conflagration, sometimes it extinguishes one; is warm and is cold, carries away or sets down, hollows out or builds up, tears or establishes, fills or empties, raises itself or burrows down, speeds or is still; is the cause at times of life or death, or increase or privation, nourishes at times and at others does the contrary; at times has a tang, at times is without

---

11   Martin, Baross, et al., "Hydrothermal Vents and the Origin of Life."
12   Douglas, *DNA Nanoscience*, 339.

savor, sometimes submerging the valleys with great floods. In time and with water, everything changes.[13]

He shows us quite clearly that water is a real paradox.

Modern Occult Themes

There are many modern occult practices that have their basis in ancient practices and beliefs. Just like the lore and themes from the past, these focus heavily on the element of water. This can be water used in a multitude of ways, including healing, divination, or in ritual.

Mesmer and Blavatsky

While religion and science have been focused on water for a very long time, the same is also true of magic. German doctor Franz Mesmer (1734–1815) is credited with the practice of mesmerism, which is known to be a forerunner of modern hypnosis. Much of Mesmer's work was focused on flow, in both the universe and directly on individuals. Towards the end of his career, Mesmer began using magnetized water as a healing remedy for his patients. He created this by using a large magnet or even just a simple wave of his hand.[14]

Famous psychic Madame Blavatsky (1831–1891), also known as Helena Blavatsky, was also very interested in water, specifically primeval water or "the water of space," as she called it. She thought it to be representative of the feminine or universal mother energy. There is one amusing story about when she was in India and filled a bottle up with water by simply putting it under her skirts. In the

---

13   Bedau and Cleland, *The Nature of Life*, 331.
14   Amao, *Healing Without Medicine*, 1.

tradition of Theosophy, of which she was one of the founders, water is said to manifest on three different levels: primordial, cosmic, and chemical.[15]

Thelemites and Water

The ritual usage of the element of water within the Thelemic path might not be as pronounced as one would imagine. But it is no less important to the everyday Thelemite, many of whom are practicing magicians either in a solitary or group capacity and participate in its rituals and ceremonies. In the Thelemic pantheon, the deity most closely related to the element of water is the goddess Nuit. In the ancient Egyptian religion, which Thelema heavily relies on, Nuit is the goddess of the sky, the stars, the cosmos, mothers, astronomy, and the entire universe.

The goddess Tefnut (deity of moisture, moist air, dew, and rain) mated with the god Shu (deity of air, wind, peace, and lions) and gave birth to the sky as the deity Nuit. She is often depicted as a nude star-covered woman arching over the earth and is described as having the image of a water pot above her head. Nuit is often portrayed within the inside lid of a sarcophagus in order to protect the dead. The vaults of the tombs were often painted dark blue as a representation of the star goddess.

In *The Book of the Dead,* it is written:

> Hail, thou Sycamore tree of the goddess Nut! Give me of the water and of the air which is in thee. I embrace that throne which is in Unu, and I keep guard over the Egg of Nekek-ur. It flourisheth, and I flourish; it liveth, and I live;

15   Blavatsky, *The Secret Doctrine*, 68.

it snuffeth the air, and I snuff the air, I the Osiris Ani, whose word is truth, in peace.[16]

Though the goddess Nuit does not have a direct attribution to the element of water, it is inferred by the attributes passed on from her parents. Nuit is also said to have given birth to the deity Nephthys, who is seen as the goddess of water and of rivers.

On a more day-to-day practice, the magician performs daily rituals of the pentagram and hexagram. The rituals of the pentagram in Western mysticism are fundamental training practices that relate to the microcosmic world, which also encompasses elemental energies. The pentagram itself represents each of the five elements. During the performance of the Greater Ritual of the Pentagram, the practitioner is required to invoke the specific pentagram representing its corresponding element. In the case of water, the practitioner stands in the west and starts drawing the pentagram of water at the point of the pentagram representing air, next drawing a line across to the point of the pentagram representing water, then down to the point of earth.

To banish the pentagram of water, the practitioner would start at the point of the pentagram representing water, draw a line across to the point of air, then down to the point of fire. The hexagram rituals are related to the macrocosm of the wider world. The hexagram represents a true union of opposites and of manifestation. The hexagram is represented by two triangles; in its classic form, there is the red triangle that has its apex pointing upright and represents the element of fire, and the blue triangle that has its apex pointing downward represents the element of water. Regardless of

---

16 Budge, *The Book of the Dead*, 109.

Thelema not having specific rituals or practices that solely encompass the element of water, the element itself is vital as a component and attribute of many for the rituals and ceremonies that a Thelemite would customarily perform.

• • • •

Water and Taino Culture

The following essay about the element of water in Taino culture is from guest contributor Miguel Sague. Miguel A. Sague Jr. (Sobaoko Koromo "Black Ribs,") was born in 1951 in Santiago, Cuba, in the eastern region of the island that is famous for its history of Taino indigenous presence. At the age of ten, he immigrated with his family to the United States, and they settled in the northeastern city of Erie, Pennsylvania. At the age of nineteen, while beginning his art college career, he began to practice the shamanic tradition of his indigenous ancestors. In 1977 Miguel collaborated with local young Native Americans to campaign for the establishment of a Native American Day in Erie. With his newlywed wife, later that year he moved to Pittsburgh, Pennsylvania, to become an employee of the Council of Three Rivers American Indian Center, where he worked to develop a Native American–themed educational curriculum. He collaborated with other Pittsburgh Tainos in 1981 to found the Caney Indigenous Spiritual Circle, a shamanic community that promoted ancient Taino spirituality. By 2015 he wrote his book *Canoa: Taino Indigenous Dream River Journey*.

MY PEOPLE, THE Taino indigenous natives of the ancient Caribbean island region, have always believed in a female divinity that is identified very closely with both the earth and with earthly waters.

The name of this divinity is Atabey, and she represents the supreme female element of the Taino pantheon. Atabey is typically represented as a maternal personality, the mother of the supreme male divinity Yokahu (the spirit of life and energy). She is also identified as the source of all creation, from whose womb emerges all that exists through terrestrial caves. She manifests in several forms and one of these forms is an entity called Itiba Cahubaba. The term *itiba* is derived from Arawak, the ancestral South American tropical rainforest regional language from which the Taino speech is descended. That word suggests bodies of water such as lakes.

As the mother of all the waters, Atabey not only represents the surface waters such as lakes, but in a different manifestation called Guabancex she is identified with violent and destructive natural phenomena such as hurricanes. In that manifestation she commands two male companions; one is Guatauba and the other is Coatriskie. Guatauba is associated with thunder, and Coatriskie represents the forces that gather torrential rain and allow it to manifest in the form of catastrophic flooding.

Caves are identified in Taino cosmology as the source place of all creation, the conduit to the divine womb. Taino belief recognizes an intimate relationship between the interior of caves and the access to the sacred underworld from which everything originates. The sacred underworld is not only the maternal uterine source place, but also the divine recycling place where all that dies returns to be reformed and then sent back out into existence. This divine recycling center is envisioned as an underground watery realm that in many ways suggests a primordial ocean where the souls of dead people can exist in a variety of forms, including fish as well as cave-dwelling bats. The divine underworld is called Coaibai, and it is perceived as a realm inhabited by the revered departed ancestors. The essence of those ancestors have the capacity to be reborn as new people within a kind of reincarnation paradigm, and yet their presence in Coaibai in their original identity still remains there forever. The flooded underworld has always manifested itself in the Caribbean indigenous consciousness within the imagery of huge sinkholes that exist on a number of locations across the Caribbean. In Kiskeya (Dominican Republic) there is a particularly significant site called Manantial de la Aleta. It contains an enormous sinkhole with a deep pool of water at the bottom. The place was used by my Taino ancestors as a site of ceremony and reverence. They came there to offer gifts to the ancient forbears, tossing valuable wooden sculptures, baskets filled with offerings, and beautifully incised gourds into the water far below. These objects have been discovered and studied by modern researchers who have explored the site in diving suits. The site suggests a vision of Taino cosmology, the vertical shaft of the sinkhole representing the cosmic central axis tree with its roots deep in the watery underworld, its branches high in the sky and its trunk rising through the earth plane where we live.

Another way in which the identity of the primordial cave is associated with water is the fact that the spirit of gentle regenerative showers, a deity called Boinayel, dwells in a legendary cave. Boinayel is identified with the vital rainwaters that begin to fall predictably during the opening of the wet season in the springtime, bringing fertility to the earth and the ability to start cultivating the life-giving food plants in the village gardens. This cave in which Boinayel is said to exist has an interesting name: Iguanaboina. The name contains an obvious linguistic reference to reptilian morphology (iguana) and has been identified with the Arawak language term "the brown serpent." The ancient Taino are known to have recognized a connection between the great All Mother, Atabey, and serpents. Our Taino ancestors inherited the reverence for snakes and the identification between snakes and the supreme maternal deity from their South American rainforest forebears who originally migrated from the Orinoco River region of Venezuela and Guyana into the Caribbean Island region thousands of years ago.

The South American anaconda snake, a gigantic constrictor whose habitat includes lakes and streams, is considered a kind of divinity by some of the indigenous people of the Orinoco River Basin. In the legends of at least two Orinoco region tribes, the primordial anaconda snake is identified with a maternal entity within whose body the germinal version of humanity is conceived and brought to earth. In the creation narrative of those two tribes, the ancestral people actually journey along the waterways of the Orinoco River rainforest region within the maternal womb of the divine snake until they are finally released into the earthly realm. In the case of one legend, they are deposited upon the riverbank in the form of fish eggs before finally hatching into the first humans. It should be remembered that this South American mainland Orinoco River region is the origin place from where the ancestors of the Taino first emigrated in canoes out to the Caribbean islands. In the creation narrative of my island-dwelling Taino ancestors, there is a reference to an emergence of all humanity from a great cave called Casibahagua. This story suggests the concept of a birth from the womb of the All Mother via her subterranean birth canal and an appearance into the world out from the flooded, watery underworld of Coaibay.

Water is perceived in our Taino ancestral tradition as the fundamental element that supports all life. In that regard the ancient indigenous perception of water very closely reflects modern-day scientific views on the nature of this fundamental liquid substance.

Miguel Sague

• • • •

Water finds its way into the creation stories and myths of almost every culture on earth. In some it is there in the beginning, and in others it is warned that it will be there in the end. These tales tell of water's power, beauty, and supreme potential. They illustrate the important lessons that are present in the watery depths. In their cultural commonality, the universal magic of water becomes clear.

Chapter 2

MYTHOLOGICAL WATERY BEASTS AND PLACES

Water can hold many powerful mysteries and treasures; some of these show up in the form of sea beasts and creatures. The majority of these creatures are formidable and larger than life, and they tell of the dangers and formidable power of water. Traditionally, these were time-tested stories told to children and others, primarily to make sure they treated the waters around them with respect, care, and caution.

In this chapter you will find just about everything from ashrays to water nymphs. There are watery beasts that seem to come either from someone's wildest dreams or worst nightmares. The second half of the chapter is dedicated to mythical places. Featuring sunken cities and even a lost continent, the opportunity is given to examine what lies beneath.

Mythological Watery Beasts

Ashrays: These Scottish creatures are said to be translucent and unable to survive on land. Some believe them to be fairies (or fair folk, as they prefer to be called). They take on the appearance of young men or women and spend their lives underwater. They are also completely nocturnal and if exposed to sunlight are said to quickly melt into a puddle.

Bäckahästen: The word *bäckahästen* translates roughly to the words "brook horse."[17] These mystical horses are from the German and Scandinavian traditions and are said to reside in brooks and rivers, luring passersby into the water.

Bunyip: A mythical water beast found in the stories of indigenous Australians, the bunyip is quite terrifying. It is said to make its home in the swamps, creeks, riverbeds, and waterholes of Australia. Described as both aggressive and very hairy, it has a great fondness for human flesh (especially that of young women and children). As if its gruesome appearance wasn't enough, the scary beast is also thought to possess great magical powers. In some stories the bunyip is said to be the original source of evil on the planet.

Chessie: Similar to Nessie, Chessie is the sea monster that is said to reside in Chesapeake Bay in the United States. There have been numerous reports of sightings over the years, and in 1982 a couple even captured the creature on video. It is said to resemble a great sea serpent with a hump on its back.[18]

Fossie Grim: In Scandinavian countries some see the Fossie Grim (also Fossegrim) as a handsome water spirit who is said to lure people to a watery grave with his delightful violin music. Others uphold that this is a beneficial energy that can bestow

---

17   Eason, *Fabulous Creatures*, 146.
18   Boffey, "Chessie Back in the Swim Again."

blessings. Fossie Grim are said to be partial to waterfalls, which are their sacred spaces. Their appearance takes the form of fair-haired youth whose feet meld into the watery foam found at the base of the waterfall. In addition to the violin, they are said to be adept at playing the harp, and those wishing to master that instrument can leave them offerings at the water.

Grindylows: Grindylows have long, thin arms and long, bony fingers. The grindylows are known to use these scary limbs to drag children and others down to the watery depths. They appear in myths and folktales from Lancashire and Yorkshire in England. There is even a grindylow in the popular Harry Potter series, which has introduced this folkloric beast to a whole new generation.

Hippocamp: In Greek mythology the hippocamp was a formidable sea creature with the head of a horse and the tail of a fish or dolphin. A team of these beasts is said to have the honor of pulling Poseidon's chariot.

Jenny Greenteeth: This formidable figure comes to us from British folktales and legends. Lurking at the bottom of lakes and ponds, this creepy sea hag is said to pull unsuspecting children to their death. Sometimes she is seen as a fairy. Most of her stories date from the nineteenth century. There are similar stories about Peg Powler, a green-skinned water witch also from England and the surrounding areas. Some say that Greenteeth specifically inhabited lakes that were covered in the plant duckweed. In fact, in some areas the common name of duckweed is Jenny Greenteeth.[19]

---

19   Vickery, "Lemna Minor and Jenny Greenteeth."

Kappas: Kappas appear in Japanese mythology and are seen as water goblins or vampires. They are said to be the size of a nine- or ten-year-old child yet are incredibly strong. There are some reports of them looking a bit like monkeys. By all accounts they are terrifying and occupy lakes, rivers, streams, and oceans. Kappas are said to attack livestock and horses, sucking the blood from their anuses. If you meet one, you must be polite and well mannered; it may also help to offer it a cucumber with your name carved into it.[20]

Kelpie: The water horses of Celtic legend are called kelpie. Residing near freshwater lakes, rivers, and streams, they have the ability to shapeshift whenever they choose. Like many shapeshifters, they can use this ability to seduce humans. They can be identified, however, by the remains of seaweed in their hair.

Kraken: Hailing from the lands of Iceland and Norway, the kraken is the infamous giant octopus. The earliest sightings of the beast date back to the thirteenth century. Since then it has been a star of literature and screen. The kraken appears in works by Herman Melville, Jules Verne, and even H. P. Lovecraft. It is probably best remembered because of the line in the 1981 film *Clash of the Titans* to "release the kraken." The word itself means "unhealthy animal," which they certainly are, being covered with tentacles, spikes, and suckers.[21]

In a letter from Herman Melville to Nathaniel Hawthorne in 1851, Melville writes:

---

20 Eiichirô, "The 'Kappa' Legend."
21 Newton, *Hidden Animals*, 83.

Lord, when shall we be done growing? As long as we have anything more to do, we have done nothing. So, now, let us add Moby Dick to our blessing, and step from that. Leviathan is not the biggest fish;—I have heard of Krakens.[22]

Leviathan: Leviathan is a sea serpent of epic proportions. It appears in the Bible in the Old Testament, and even before that in Mesopotamian myths and in a Canaanite poem from ancient Ugarit. Oftentimes it is depicted as a serpent or water dragon, but in ancient Hungary there are legends that describe it as a whale. By all accounts it is a monster, and a dangerous beast at that.

In the book of Job in the King James version of the Bible, it says,

Canst thou draw out leviathan with an hook? or his tongue with a cord which thou lettest down?...Out of his mouth go burning lamps, and sparks of fire leap out. Out of his nostrils goeth smoke, as out of a seething pot or cauldron. His breath kindleth coals, and a flame goeth out of his mouth.[23]

Some early Kabbalists equate tales of the leviathan and its mate with Samael and Lilith, probably because of its depiction as a serpent.

Lorelei: Also spelled Loreley, this name is given both to a cliff that sits above the Rhine River and a mythical spirit of the sea. In some tales she is called the maiden or the queen of the Rhine, and she can be depicted as benevolent or treacherous, much like the river itself. Her earliest appearance in literature was in the mid-eighteenth century. She later became famous in 1801

22   Parker, *Herman Melville*, 865.
23   The Holy Bible (King James Version), Job 41.

when German author Brentano expanded the legend of Lorelei with his *Zu Bacharach am Rheine*.[24]

Mermaids, Mermen, and Merfolk: Merfolk have been in existence for thousands of years. They are featured in the sacred stories and myths of Africa, Indonesia, Europe, Australia, New Zealand, Asia, and the Americas. Some of the earliest recorded evidence of these watery people date back to around 200 BCE with Oannes of the early Babylonians. Oannes was said to have the complete body of a fish but also the head and feet of a man. In his contact with humans, he gave them great knowledge and helped them create dwellings and also gather food and resources. He was said to return to the sea each night to sleep.

One of the most popular tales of merfolk is one of Scandinavian or possibly German origin called "Agnes and the Merman." The date for the original story is unclear, but in it is the line:

Agnes she walked on the edge of the steep,
And up came a Merman out from the deep.—Ha ha.[25]

Agnes was captured by this merman and brought down below the waters, where she birthed seven of his sons. One day he agreed to let her go back to the land to go to church, but she does not return. The story is immortalized in a series of sculptures in Copenhagen called "Agnete and the Mermen."

However, the most famous mermaid tale of all is *The Little Mermaid* written by Hans Christian Andersen in 1837. It draws on folklore and mythology from earlier times such as "Agnes and the Merman" and "Undine," which was written in

---

24   Mustard, "Siren-Mermaid."
25   Waugh, "The Folklore of the Merfolk."

1811 by Freidrich de la Motte Fouqué.[26] In the story, the mermaid rescues a drowning prince and takes him safely to land. She wishes to return to him and live on the land. In order to do this, she must strike a bargain with the sea witch and relinquish her beautiful voice. Andersen here presents the iconic figure of the sea witch, saying:

> The sea witch's house sat in a strange forest. It was surrounded by bushes that were half plant and half animal. They looked like wriggling snakes with hundreds of heads and slimy, wormlike fingers. If those fingers caught something, they would never let go.[27]

Another condition is that in order to keep her soul (or gain one), she must make the prince fall madly in love with her. The mermaid's efforts are complicated and mostly futile, and her mermaid sisters urge her to kill the prince. She is unable to do this and throws herself into the sea, where she is lifted up to the realm of the immortals.

Christopher Columbus reported seeing mermaids on his journey in 1492, and in 1614 Captain John Smith made similar reports.[28] There are mermaids from Scotland that are said to rise from the sea to tell people about the healing powers of mugwort, among other things. In Java there is the mermaid goddess Loro Kidul (also known as Nyai Roro Kidul), called the bride of the endless sea. Most myths say that this goddess was born a princess who was cursed by an evil stepmother or a jealous wife and given leprosy or another skin disease. Because of this

26   Mortensen, "The Little Mermaid: Icon and Disneyfication."
27   Sarah Hines-Stephens, retold from Hans Christian Andersen, *The Little Mermaid and Other Stories*, 19.
28   Banse, "Mermaids."

disease she fled into the forest, where she heard the voices of spirits who told her she could regain her former beauty if she threw herself into the sea. Once in the sea, she was elevated to the level of queen and goddess. It is said that the color green is hers, and travelers in Indonesia are cautioned not to wear this color, as she may be called to take them to the sea to live with her. The people in the area are highly respectful of her legacy; in fact, there is even a room reserved for her permanently in the Samudra Beach Hotel in Pelabuhan Ratu, Java, where room 308 is forever reserved for her, decorated with her favorite colors of green and gold and scented with jasmine. If you would like to see it for yourself, visitors are permitted to reserve the room for meditation sessions.

Here in my hometown of Brooklyn, New York, is probably the most famous display of mermaids anywhere in the form of the Mermaid Parade. Thousands of people dress in their finest mermaid gear and parade through the streets near the beach at Coney Island. It allows people to flaunt their wet and wild goodness that comes from the sea.

Naiads, Nymphs, and Sprites: In both Greek and Roman mythology we find reference to water naiads, nymphs, and sprites. They are seen as otherworldly beings that are specifically associated with a watery locale, such as fountains, wells, and streams. Nymphs, however, could be found on either land or water.

Nereids: Nereids are sea nymphs immortalized in both literature and myth. They are said to be the fifty daughters of Nereus and Doris and are an important component in religious thought in Greek history. Appearing in art as early as the fourth century BCE, they are frequently shown riding sea creatures such as dolphins. Some theorists, such as Barringer, have posited that they serve as a metaphor for journeys, specifically both marriage and death.[29]

Nessie: Nessie, or the Loch Ness Monster, is arguably the most infamous sea creature of all. Despite any concrete evidence, there have been over a thousand sightings of this watery creature said to reside in Loch Ness in Scotland. Some believe it to be an eel or even a prehistoric reptile.

Rusalka: Rusalka are female ghosts that come to us through Slavic mythology. Most often they are water maidens similar to sirens and mermaids whose objective is to drive individuals under the water to their death.

Scylla: Scylla is the word used to describe a mythological creature and also the location where this creature resides. That place is generally thought to be the narrow strait of Messina between Calabria and Sicily. The other side of the strait was said to be inhabited by the dangerous beast Charybdis. The expression "between Scylla and Charybdis"[30] comes from these tales and means an individual is caught between two very difficult dangers. Described as a canine beast, Scylla is the daughter of Hecate, according to some. She is described in the classical literature of Apollodorus, Apollonius, Ovid, and Homer. In Ovid's take, Scylla is a water nymph who was poisoned in a sea pool by a jealous rival. This poisoning results in her gruesome transformation. She is depicted in classical art by painters J. M. W.

---

29 Barringer, "Europa and the Nereids: Wedding or Funeral?"
30 "Between Scylla and Charybdis," *Encyclopedia Britannica*, last modified June 10, 2019, https://www.britannica.com/topic/Scylla-and-Charybdis.

Turner, John William Waterhouse, Agostino Carracci, and others.

Selkies: Selkies are one of the most popular beings of Celtic mythology. They are featured in many folktales, books, games, and even a few films. Selkies are shapeshifters, most often assuming the form of seals. They are said to reside in underwater caves in the waters surrounding the Orkney and Shetland Islands. Unlike many of the creatures described in this book, selkies are thought to be beneficial beings who can be helpful in their interactions with humans. Some legends state that they are the souls of drowned individuals, while others see them as angels fallen out of heaven but too pure for hell. The selkies are said to take human lovers. Crying seven tears into the sea is believed to be one way to call them. If they have found love, selkies often make the decision to discard their seal skins and live on land.

Sirens: There is an intoxicating song that can be heard on the seas; it is the song of sirens. But what exactly are these beings? Depending on where and when they are found, sirens can be human or otherworldly; they may lure you to your death or give you the delicious kiss of everlasting life.

These siren stories and sightings appear throughout the world. In Central and South America, the "Weeping Woman," called La Llorona, occasionally appears on water too. In Mexico, in particular, there is a story of a woman whose child drowned in a lake, and now she appears in that lake, luring lovers to her and laughing as they both go down under the water to the deadly depths.

One of the earliest artistic representations of sirens is the Siren Vase housed in the British Museum. This Greek vase dates from approximately 480 BCE and features the ship of Odysseus passing the sirens. These sirens are winged beings with female heads.

In the thirteenth century, Guillaume le Clerc de Normandie wrote of these beings in his *Bestiaries and Lapidaries*:

> The siren is a monster of strange fashion, for from the waist up it is the most beautiful thing in the world, formed in the shape of a woman. The rest of the body is like a fish or a bird. So sweetly and beautifully does she sing that they who go sailing over the sea, as soon as they hear the song, cannot keep from going towards her. Entranced by the music, they fall asleep in their boat, and are killed by the siren before they can utter a cry.[31]

Titans: According to Greek mythology, the Titans were gods even before gods existed. They were credited with all creation. Comprising six sisters named Thea, Rhea, Themis, Mnemosyne, Phoebe, and Tethys, and six brothers called Oceanus (god of fresh water), Coeus, Hyperion, Iapetus, Crius, and Cronus, they are the children of Heaven and Earth. Of these deities, two—namely Phoebe and Themis—were said to have the gift of prophecy and were regarded as oracles.

Uncegila: This horned water serpent comes from Lakota mythology. She was said to be enormous, with shiny scales, spots, and a sparkling crest down her back. Looking at the serpent is said to bring on blindness and eventually death. One watery tale says she rose from the primal waters and flooded the land. Revenge

31   Warner, *The Library of the World's Best Literature*.

for this destruction was enacted by Thunderbird, who summoned a great storm with lightning that dried up the water and sent Uncegila to her death.

Vodianoi: The vodianoi are said to be old men with green beards, covered in hair, scales, and slime. Slavic in origin, they are said to live underwater inside sunken ships.

Mythological Watery Places

Water is so powerful it is no wonder that there are numerous mythological places that are intricately connected to the element. There are magical healing isles, as well as sunken cities and even an underwater continent. Each contains its own magic, lore, and deep mystery.

Atlantis: The origin of this famed lost civilization traces back to Plato and his dialogues the *Timaeus* and the *Critias*, written around 360 BCE. The city was said to be a paradise filled with elaborate constructions, geological treasures, and exotic flora and fauna. The society there became greedy and corrupt, and the gods sent violent fires and earthquakes, after which it sunk to the depths of the sea. While no respectable scientists now believe that the place actually existed, it does serve as an elaborate cautionary tale as to what can happen if people get too out of hand. In Plato's works Atlantis is seen as the antithesis of Athens, which was said to be ruled with modesty, logic, and science.

Avalon: Said to be the home of the Lady of the Lake, Avalon has graced Celtic mythology for centuries. The first mention of the mythic isle in literature was by Geoffrey of Monmouth in his

Historia Regum Britanniae, or History of the Kings of Britain, written back in AD 1136. It was also called the Isle of Apples or the Isle of Glass. The location was said to have great healing powers. People there lived extraordinarily long lives and time was said to function differently in this place. It has a special connection to the dead and was also said to be the home of the legendary Morgan le Fay. Some scholars think its name Isle of Glass may have been based on the actual site of Glastonbury in England.

Lemuria: This sunken continent first got its name from English zoologist Philip L. Sclater in 1864. He used the word to describe the sunken land mass that he envisioned connected the areas of Africa, Asia, and Madagascar. Sclater proposed that Lemuria was responsible for the exotic species of animals distributed throughout the areas, such as the lemur. However, others have pointed out that Lemuria was the name of the Roman feast of the Lemures, an ancient festival for the spirits of the dead. These dead were fearsome and said to devour the souls of the living. Lemuria took place on May 9, 11, and 13, and was designed to cast out these negative energies.

Modern New Age and occult practices have taken up the banner of this locale, exclaiming that it is the source of much ancient knowledge and information. For them the place was a utopia, fertile with animals, plants, and sacred wisdom. Many believe that this was the same legendary site as the island of Mu, or even Atlantis. The people there were said to have extraordinary psychic powers and abilities. These beliefs carry over into the use of special Lemurian quartz crystals. Also known as Lemurian seed crystals or star seeds, they are seen as being able to impart the ancient knowledge of Lemurians and can be useful in accessing higher realms and also realigning and rebalancing chakras.

The interesting thing about this "lost continent" of Lemuria is that recently scientists, including Professor Lewis Ashwal at South Africa's University of the Whitwatersrand, found evidence of a continent in approximately the same location. Discovered under the popular island of Mauritius, the lava-covered piece of land was given the name Mauritia.[32]

Water in many ways represents the unknown. It can be filled with magical creatures and even mystical places. Individuals can be left chasing water dragons like Nessie or searching for lost places like Lemuria. This watery unknown is a liminal space, a place of in-between where things are not always what they seem.

---

32 Wits University, "Researchers confirm the existence of a 'lost continent' under Mauritius," https://phys.org/news/2017-01 -lost-continent-mauritius.html.

Chapter 3

WATER AND
THE DIVINE

There are many deities that take as their domain all different forms of water. Deities exist for lakes, streams, wells, rivers, oceans, and every manifestation of water in between. Their corresponding energies can be hot or cold, steamy, or even magically dreamy. Some belong to a specific watery locale, while others such as Mami Wata represent the sacred energy of water itself.

Water Goddesses, Deities, and Orishas

Like water itself, water goddesses, deities, and orishas grace every corner of the world. For many there is something inherently feminine about water. These sacred women of water come from every part of the world. Each has their own special nature, and I will do my best to examine their sacred watery powers here.

Abnoba: Abnoba is known by many names: Avnova, Dianae Abnobae, Dea Abnoba, Abna, and Abnova. She is a water goddess whose domain is the sacred waters that flow in the Black

Forest region of Germany. Historically this has been considered a place of great magic and mystery. I have visited there and completely agree. Some say the origins of her name may be similar to that of the word Avon, both of which mean "river."

Amberella: Hailing from Lithuania, Amberella is an ocean goddess. She bestows gifts of amber from the sea to those who honor her. She is said to help with issues of love, fertility, and money.

Amphitrite: Amphitrite is a Greek goddess known for dominion over the ocean. She is said to be the consort of Poseidon and resides in a cave beneath the sea.

Anahita: Anahita is a Persian goddess in charge of fertility and feminine mysteries. It is said that she is pulled in a chariot with four different horses representing rain, wind, clouds, and sleet. Associated with lakes, rivers, and all waters, she especially presides over the magical waters of birth. The Greek pantheon associates her with Aphrodite, while she also has connections with Ishtar, Astarte, Athena, and Anat. Her name roughly translates to mean "the immaculate one."

Aphrodite: Most often Aphrodite is seen as the Greek goddess of love and desire. In the Roman pantheon her counterpart is Venus. She is said to govern beauty, art, pleasure, sensuality, and fertility. The mythological tale of her birth is an interesting one. It is said that she arose fully formed from the sea after the castration of the god Ouranos, her father. The word *aphrodisiac* comes from her name, as she has the power to enchant on every level. Her animal spirit companion is most often a dove.

Atanensic: Known as Sky Woman, Ataensic, Ata-en-sic, Ataentsic, Atahensic, Ataensiq, Aataentsic, and other names, this goddess comes to us from the indigenous Huron and Iroquois people of North America. Her myths say she fell through a hole in the skies and was rescued by sea birds, set on the back of a turtle, and delivered to her current home of Turtle Island. She is said to be associated with marriages, fertility, and traditionally female crafts and creations.

Bai Tanki: Bai Tanki is an Indian goddess whose tragedy forms an extreme mythic story. It is said many men tried to rape her as a young woman and she sought the aid of magic to come to her rescue. It is here that sexually transmitted diseases were born. As each attacker tried to assault her, his penis became diseased; despite this, one evil individual was successful. Her pain and sorrow caused her to transform into a river and spread these maladies throughout the earth.

Berba: Berba, along with Eoryus and Suirus, are the "three sisters" that govern the rivers of Southeast Ireland. Specifically, Berba is said to be the goddess of the Barrow River.

Boann: Also known as the "White Cow," this deity is the resident goddess of the Boyne River in Ireland. Located near the sacred ancient tombs of Newgrange, Knowth, and Dowth, the river is a source of both power and mystery. Like the goddess Sinann, Boann tested the boundaries of the water and met a watery death. It is said she broke a taboo concerning the sacred well there and looked into the sacred water. Boann is said to be a patron of poets, creativity, fertility, knowledge, and divine inspiration. Boann was the daughter of Delbáeth of the Tuatha dé Danann.

Brigit: Her name roughly translates to "fiery one" in the ancient language of the Celts, which refers to her connections to sacred flame. However, she is also associated with healing water and springs. She is also the patron deity of prophecy, the hearth, poets, midwives, sailors, travelers, and even fugitives. Many varying animals fall under her powerful protection, particularly lambs, bees, cows, snakes, and also owls.

Chalchihuitlicue: This deity is from ancient Mexico, dating back to the time even before the Aztec occupation. She is a young and sensual goddess whose domain is flowing water. She has the power to both give life-sustaining water and to flood, creating destruction. Her name roughly means "lady of the green skirt" and refers to her connection to the stone jade. She is often depicted wearing watery colors like green and blue and has water lily flowers in her hair. She is also said to have a blue nose ring with serpents on each end. Chalchihuitlicue's connection to water is apparent, as it is said she caused great torrential rains and dangerous whirlpools to come and flood the earth for decades, yet she also is said to have spared humans by transforming them into fish so they could survive. Her waters are said to be necessary, bringing both cleansing and healing. She is also often associated with the snake and is seen as a protector of children and fishermen.

Coventina: An ancient Roman goddess, she is said to preside over the sacred spring near Hadrian's Wall in Britain. Excavations at the site have uncovered two images of the goddess where she is shown as a water nymph holding a jug or a beaker.

Ehuang: This Chinese goddess is connected to the River Qiantang. It is said that she threw herself into the river and transformed into the goddess of daffodils.

Erzulie: Erzulie, or Ezili, technically isn't a goddess but is instead a lwa from the Haitian Vodou and New Orleans Voodoo pantheon. To make matters even more complex, there isn't just one Erzulie; there are legions of them. Each one occupies their own unique space in the traditions. Erzulie is said to rule over the ritual baths that occur each year at Saut-d'Eau in Haiti.

Erzulie Danto: This Erzulie is fierce. She is seen as a powerful mother who protects her children and also makes sure they live correctly. Erzulie Danto is seen as hardworking and typically is honored with the colors red and blue. The customary offerings for this Haitian lwa are numerous. Most notably she likes silver chains, necklaces, jewelry, rum, creme de cacao, perfume, red wine, unfiltered cigarettes, dark-skinned dolls, and small daggers. Veves (ritual drawings) for her often feature this dagger piercing a heart.

Erzulie Freda Dahomey: This Haitian lwa is often seen as crying tears that rain down on behalf of humanity. Erzulie Freda Dahomey wants people to act better and to be better. This lwa is syncretized with Mater Dolorosa, her favorite colors are said to be pink and light blue, and her ritual number is most often seven. For offerings she loves to receive sweet champagne and pastries. The veve (ritual drawing) for her frequently has curls or frills around the edge, mimicking lace.

Ganga: Ganga is the Hindu goddess of the River Ganges. Half of her is said to reside in the river, the other half in the Milky Way. She is said to wash away all past and present karmas. She can purify, heal, and energize one's body and soul.

Idemili: Idemili is the deity of the Idemili River in Nigeria. She is said to offer protection for women in childbirth, mothers, and infants, and is said to defend them fiercely. Classified as a divinity of the Igbo people, she is also associated with snakes and pythons, many of which are found in her river. There are many shrines dedicated to her, and she is one of the most popular water deities in the area.

Isis: Isis is one of the most popular of all the goddesses. She has been honored for approximately 4500 years (with origin dates varying from 2700–2500 BCE). She was both a goddess and a queen, whose worship was born in Egypt, specifically the Nile River Valley. Isis is a mother goddess who represents all things maternal and feminine. Her sacred domain is one of beauty, love, abundance, marriage, fertility, healing, the power of the moon, and the mysteries of the afterlife. Goddess Isis's power is known by many names: Aset, Ast, Usert, and Eset are just a few. Amethyst, bloodstone, coral, emerald, lapis lazuli, moonstone, ruby, and turquoise are the crystals and gemstones associated with her. Animals sacred to Isis are cows, lions, scorpions, cats, and the sphinx. Her most sacred symbol is the ankh; this is similar to the ritual amulets made for her from bloodstone known as the "Isis knot."

Julunggul: This indigenous Australian goddess features prominently in their creation myths. She is a rainbow-colored serpent
representative of both rainwater and seawater. Julunggul has
the ability to manifest as a lightning storm.

Jurate: This goddess is said to be queen of the mermaids in Lithu-
anian folktales. She is seen as constantly weeping precious tears
of amber. Her primary role is that of healing.

Juturna: An ancient Roman goddess, Juturna is said to have been
the patron of springs, fountains, wells, and rivers. Her day of
celebration, called Juturnalia, is January 11. She appears in
the works of Virgil, Ovid, and other classical writers. Juturna
is known to be connected with both immortality and healing,
which could be granted with her holy waters.

Keto: This Greek goddess, also called Ceto, is said to be the queen
of sea monsters.

Korrigans: Like many of the water deities described here, the Korrigans were dangerous. They were said to attract their victims
by dancing each night before proceeding to drown them. They
are found most often in Celtic lore, specifically that of Brittany.

Kymopoleia: In the Greek pantheon Kymopoleia, or Cymopoleia,
was a sea-dwelling nymph who was wed to the storm giant Bri-
areos. She is said to rule over the fierce waves that occur during
a storm.

La Sirenn: In the religion of Haitian Vodou there is a lwa named
La Sirenn or Lasirene. Her domain is the sea. La Sirenn is said
to be the wife of Agwe. Very often pictured as a mermaid, she
is known to sing songs of truth and lies. She is offered jewelry

(often diamonds and pearls), mirrors, combs, sweet fruit, and drink. Some of the veves (sacred drawings) for her feature a mermaid.

Mami Wata: Many of the goddesses on this list have dominion over their specific location and the sacred water that flows there. This is not the case with Mami Wata. This African deity is representative of all water. Wherever you have water, Mami Wata in all her glory is there. Artistic representations frequently show Mami Wata as a mermaid, and a double-tailed one at that. People have likened her to some of the other orisha or lwa that represent water. The orisha Oshún is indeed the ashe of the river, but Mami Wata is the sacred energy of *all* water, including rivers. In Benin there are several groups that honor Mami Wata in their practices. There are also several individuals that align themselves with her; these people customarily have a special connection to the water and profound abilities of mediumship.

Mazu: Mazu is one of the most popular deities in China, second only to Kuan Yin. There are over a thousand temples dedicated to this goddess of sailors and people who fish. Also known by the names Heavenly Empress, Heavenly Princess, and Holy Mother, the name *Mazu* itself roughly translates to the word "granny." Again there is this connection between the ancient feminine and water. Worship of Mazu dates back to approximately the year 1000 CE. In addition, she is still worshiped in modern times and even appeared on a postage stamp that debuted in 1992. Her worship has spread far and wide, and she is present not only in China but Japan, Taiwan, other parts of Asia, and even Europe and the Americas. Each one is slightly different and has taken on the unique character of the people and place where they reside.

Legends tell us that Mazu was an actual girl, a magical and silent one who was called Lin Moniang and born in Meizhou. As a child she had amazing powers and was said to have had contact with water spirits who gifted her with the special power of being able to save those in peril on the sea. She is also said to have been able to heal the sick, bring rain to needy crops, and exorcise demons. When she died at a young age—in her twenty-seventh or twenty-eighth year—she continued to have worshipers and her popularity grew exponentially. She went on to become a state-sanctioned goddess. It has been suggested that this move was calculated to help the local governments get control of some of the energy that surrounded her worship and convert it for their own ends.

Miriam: Miriam is mentioned in the Bible as a sister of Moses and a great prophetess. It is said that she led the women in dance at the sea of reeds. Today many feminists have taken up her cause and sing to her on Saturday night as part of their worship. Legends say that a well of water followed Miriam through the wilderness to satisfy the thirst of the people and that the well also grew herbs that were useful for healing.

Morrigan: The Morrigan are Irish river goddesses associated with the River Unius. She is sometimes portrayed as a single goddess and at other times a trifold divinity. Her name means "great phantom queen." She is seen as a warrior whose great weapon is magic. History has connected her with the Lamia, terrifying night demons who are also associated with the ancient goddess

Lilith. Her totemic bird is the crow, associated with magic, death, and mystery.

Nanshe: This Sumerian goddess, also called Nanse or Nance, rules over divination and also social justice. She is said to be skilled at interpreting dreams and messages. She is immortalized in *A Hymn to Nanse*, which is believed to date to approximately 2100 BCE.[33] The center of her worship was in Lagash, which is now known as Southeastern Iraq.

Obba: Obba, also known as Oba, is the orisha of the river of the same name in the Oyo and Osun States in Nigeria. She is found in both the Ifá pantheon and the religion of La Regla Lucumi. She is said to be one of the wives of Changó. There are numerous versions of patakí (sacred instructional stories) about her, but the most famous involves an accusation, either real or imaginary, that she cut off her ears and fed them to her husband. This act brought about great sadness and mistrust.

Olokun: Olokun is the orisha of the deep sea found in African traditional religions. About Olokun it is said that "no one knows what lies at the bottom of the ocean." Olokun is said to be the mysteries of these murky depths. The orisha can provide you with great wealth and success or cart you off to a watery demise. In many spiritual houses Olokun is seen as a counterpart to Yemayá, and initiations frequently incorporate the ashe (sacred energy) of both orishas.

---

33 Maxwell-Hyslop, "The Goddess Nanše."

Oshún: Oshún is the orisha of the river. She is said to rule over money, gold, marriage, beauty, dance, and other delightful areas. Most often she is represented by statues of Caridad del Cobre, Our Lady of Copper, whose feast day is celebrated on September 8. Oshún's ritual colors are yellow and gold, and her altars are frequently draped in elaborate fabrics. The patakí (sacred instructional story) that explains this tells of a time when the orisha was short on money and had fallen on difficult times despite her status as queen. Consequently, she had to wash her clothes out by hand each day in the river. After repeated washings her pristine white clothes gradually turned yellow. This is why Oshún's color is said to be yellow today. The Osun River in Nigeria, along with the nearby sacred groves, is a UNESCO World Heritage site. In every way Oshún is an inspiration for creativity and loving joy.

Here is a song written by Jason Winslade, a professor and accomplished musician. This was written after some of his early encounters with this orisha in ritual and practice.

Angel of Time

She gathers water
She swims in honey
She's goddess daughter
She burns and flows in fire light

She sings your true name
She dances your story
Keeper of the cold flame
The child of gold and mystery
When darkest night is here with me
I worship her eternity
We walk alone
Through endless days
Lost in the labyrinthine maze

Time is a lover
Her kiss is hours
The scarlet mother
Gives birth to moments in between
In between

The burning waves will drive us on
Where Oshún bathes with Babalon
In Venus shell
At Brigid's well
The angel fell

And time releases ecstasy
Now and
Now

Jason Winslade

• • • •

Ran: Seen as the wife of Aegir in the Norse pantheon, Ran is a giant who rules over the sea and those who have died there. She appears with black hair and teal-colored skin and is also known to manifest as a mermaid. The sea itself was called Ran's road, and those that traveled on it were advised to leave her offerings of gold so she would not drag them with her net down into the watery depths. It is said that she is the mother of nine daughters, referred to as the wave maidens. Legend tells us that if a drowned individual's ghost appears at its own funeral, they are said to have been accepted into Ran's otherworldly realm.

Sarasvati: Sarasvati, also called Saraswati, is both a Hindu goddess and a river. She grants knowledge, wisdom, and inspiration.

Sedna: Sedna is an Inuit goddess of the sea. Also known as Sanna or Arnakuagsak, the story of her creation says she began as a woman with great beauty and many suitors. None pleased her, however, and in time she became tricked into marrying a seagull who promised her a great life. When she arrived at his home, the evils of the marriage became apparent. She sent word to her father to rescue her. After some time her parents arrived to take her away, but as they tried to leave, a great storm arose and she was thrown overboard.

Some versions of this tale say this was done by her father, others by the men who had come to assist in the rescue. In any case, as she tried to climb back into the boat, her fingers were crushed and she was sacrificed to the bottom of the sea. As she sank, her fingers were transformed into fish, walruses, whales, seals, and other sea creatures. In the depths of the sea she remains today, a guardian of all the life that lives there. This woman of the waves is known for helping with transformation and sacrifices while simultaneously providing abundance and success.

Sequana: This goddess is alternately called Siquanna or Secuana and is said to rule over the River Seine flowing through Paris and the north of France. The name literally translates as "fast-flowing one." She was known to bestow healing through her waters and springs. A healing shrine was established for her in Burgundy around the second century BCE. It was said to confer miraculous cures, especially for those having problems with their eyes or sight. Artwork depicts the pilgrims there leaving offerings of food, fruit, jewelry, money, and even their pets.

Sinann: Sinann is the ancient Celtic goddess of the Shannon River, the longest river in Ireland. Sinann, or Siona, was said to be the granddaughter of Lir, the Celtic god of the sea. She is connected to Connla's Well, which was said to contain great wisdom. The well is said to have overflowed when she tried to partake of its wisdom (either in the form of hazelnuts or salmon, depending on the retelling). This caused the water to rise and drown her, creating the Shannon River, which bears her name. This story illustrates the important theme of boundaries where water is concerned, both for safety and as an access point to the divine.

Styx: The River Styx is the water that separates the living from the dead. The goddess of the same name comes from the Greek pantheon and was one of the Oceanid sisters. The word *styx* means "shuddering," and indeed this goddess inspires fear. In Homer's great works the *Iliad* and the *Odyssey*, people swear oaths on the river itself the same way many people use Bibles today. This goddess is all about the depths of these oaths and ourselves.

Sulis: Sulis is a Celtic goddess of healing water and cleansing. She is said to be the patron of the springs in Bath, England. When the Romans arrived in Bath, she became blended with Minerva, becoming the goddess Sulis Minerva. In 1727 one of the most famous archaeological finds from Roman Britain was discovered, namely the bronze head from the statue of Sulis Minerva that most likely graced the site. The head is slightly larger than life and has six layers of gilding, the last four being gold leaf.

Tefnut: Tefnut is the ancient Egyptian goddess of humidity and moisture. Most often Tefnut appears as half human and half lion, but there are some images that depict her as a serpent coiled around a scepter. She was called the "Eyes of Ra." The left eye was said to represent the moon and the right, the sun. She is seen as the daughter of Ra and the sister and wife of Shu. Images frequently show her wearing a solar disk and an ankh.

Telphusa: Telphusa was said to be a nymph of the spring on Mount Tilphousios in Central Greece. Also known as Tilphousa or Tilphusa, she is said to be associated with the goddess Erinyes. Her name translates loosely to mean "bringing forth marsh," and this could mean that her waters were often stagnant or tainted.

Thetis: Thetis is another of the Greek sea nymphs known as the Nerieds, seen as daughters of Nereus and Doris. Her sanctuary was located in Sparta.

Tiamat: Tiamat is said to be a mother goddess or, in some cases, a grandmother goddess that is said to be the creator of all. Her name comes from the word *tamtu*, which loosely translates to the word "sea." Often she is depicted as a water dragon, both fierce and powerful. Her origins are rooted in ancient Babylon and date back to approximately 1000 BCE. She is associated with the stone amazonite. In modern times she is probably more well known as a character in Dungeons & Dragons and Final Fantasy games.

Vellamo: This Finnish water goddess is said to rule over the sea. Her name comes from the word *velloa*, which is loosely translated to mean "to rock oneself." She is known to appear as a mermaid.

Xiwang Mu: Also called Hsi-Wang-Mu, this ancient deity from China fulfills a lot of roles. Some see her as a sovereign and others, a demon. Her name means "Queen Mother of the West," and she is a most ancient deity. Legend tells us that she was a spirit from the Kunlun Mountains who transformed into a partial human, still retaining a leopard's tail and fierce tiger teeth. She is said to grow a magical garden with rare flowers, plants, and a special Saturn peach of immortality. Xiwang Mu is frequently depicted in art, where she is shown riding a crane, phoenix, or dragon. She is said to control the cosmic forces of space and time.

Yamuna: This Hindu goddess is associated with the river of the same name that is the main source of the Ganges River. In art she is seen riding a tortoise, of which there are many on the banks of her river.

Yemayá: Traditionally celebrated on September 7, this orisha is honored throughout the world. Devotees worship her in the religions of Ifá, La Regla Lucumi (Santeria), Candomble, and to some extent also in the New Orleans Voodoo tradition. Her botanical offerings include many water elemental plants: spearmint, seaweed, basil, eucalyptus, gardenia, lemon balm, lotus, and myrrh. Yemayá's sacred foods include watermelon (whole), black molasses, coconut, pineapple, fish, and others. Her ashe (sacred energy) is that of the ocean water. Wherever there is ocean water, she is present. Her sacred colors are most often blue and white, like the sea itself. Many associate her with the qualities of a mother goddess, for she can be gentle, kind, and nurturing, but turn fierce if her children are harmed.

Yewa: Yewa is an orisha in the Yoruba pantheon, seen as the wife of Orunmila. Very often she is viewed as a mysterious woman with a special connection to death; however, she is also an orisha of the river. She is therefore connected to both water and life itself. The actual Yewa River forms a boundary between the countries of Nigeria and the Republic of Benin. She is frequently assigned the color pink and the number ten.

Water Gods

In many societies water is gendered primarily as female. There are, however, a number of gods that stake their claim on a watery domain.

Aegir: This Norse god of the oceans and salt was said to have the mighty kraken as his animal.

Agwe: Agwe is the Haitian Vodou lwa embodying the ashe (sacred energy) of water and safe passage. The colors for Agwe are blue and white, and offerings of flowers, food, and beverages are left at (or in) the sea for him. Artistically Agwe is honored with a veve (sacred drawing) depicting a fishing net and a sailboat with the word *immamou* on the side.

Ah-Patnar-Unicob: There are over 250 deities in the ancient Mayan pantheon; these ones were the gods of water. They were said to have been honored during an eight-day rain ceremony.

Akheloios: Akheloios is a Greek god embodying the spirit of the Aitolia River, the largest freshwater river in the country.

Albion: Some people see Albion as an alternative or even mythological name for the land now known as Britain. Albion is also a god of the sea.

Bolon-D'zacab: Bolon-D'zacab is a Mayan agricultural deity who was said to be the keeper of seeds. He is a god of storms and lightning. In ancient images he is shown with the face of a reptile.

Chac: The Mayan supreme god of rain and lightning. He was said to preside over wells, springs, and streams. He was a very popular deity, and offerings and prayers were frequently dedicated to him. Very often he was pictured with snakes coming out of his mouth.

Enki: Enki comes to us through ancient Sumeria. He is said to have been a god of wisdom and fate, and a joyous and also terrifying ruler of seas and rivers. Here we find the age-old connections between water and sacred knowledge of both the past and future.

Glaucus: There are many individuals called Glaucus in Greek mythology, and in that language the name roughly translates to the word "gleaming." Glaucus of Anthedon was a fisherman who, upon eating some magical herbs or grasses, was transformed into a god and leaped into the sea. In other tales of him he was transformed into a merman with green skin covered with seaweed and seashells.

Haddad: Haddad is a Sumerian and Phoenician weather god. He was frequently depicted wearing horns and holding a club and a thunderbolt.

Hydros: In the Greek pantheon, Hydros is said to be a god of fresh water. He was known to be married to Thesis (creation) and Gaia (earth).

Inle: The orisha Inle, also called Erinle, is the ashe (sacred energy) of the Erinle River in Nigeria. This short river flows directly into the Osun River. He is in charge of health and healing, and his domain is the space between the river and the sea. Inle is supposed to be a great fisherman and hunter. He is syncretized with St. Raphael, whose feast day is September 29. Traditionally, Inle does not speak; instead, he delivers messages and information through the orisha Yemayá.

Manannán mac Lir: Coming to us from Celtic legend and lore is the god Manannán mac Lir. It is said that his throne was the Isle of Man, and he was known as both son of the sea and lord of the oceans. Manannán mac Lir has many magical powers and tools, including a copper boat that was said to move without sails or oars and transport you anywhere you wished.

Neptune: Neptune, or Neptunus, was originally the god of fresh water in ancient Rome. Over time he became equated with the Greek god Poseidon and shifted to domain over the sea. His festival, called Neptunalia, occurred on July 23. The name traces its origin back to words meaning "moist" or "mist." Like Poseidon, he is often featured in artwork carrying a trident. He can use this trident to create destruction like tsunamis, floods, and shipwrecks, or to calm the seas. He is said to have a fleet of dolphins as companions.

Osiris: Osiris is one of the most well-known deities in the Egyptian pantheon. There are many myths and legends surrounding him, but the first deals with his birth. The myth is known to date from the twenty-fourth century BCE or before. It is said that Osiris was the son of Geb, the earth, and Nut, the sky. Osiris grew and eventually married his sister Isis and became king of Egypt. As a ruler he was known to be wise and helpful, and he was said to command both the love and respect of his people.

His brother Set was known to rule over the desert, and Osiris's domain was that of the Nile River and its valley. Set became overcome with jealousy and plotted his downfall. According to Plutarch (approximately 46–119 CE), Osiris was either drowned or somehow slain by Set. His lifeless corpse was torn to pieces and distributed throughout the land. Isis and her sister Nephthys eventually recovered all the pieces except for the phallus. In some versions of the story, she makes another one out of gold, but, in any case, she manages to resurrect Osiris long enough to become pregnant with Horus. Osiris is then transformed into the god of the underworld, where he is said to remain. Horus eventually avenges his father's death and becomes king of Egypt.

Phorcys: Also spelled Phorkys or Phorkos, this lesser god from Greece is said to rule the sea. He is known to travel with the sea serpent Keto and is the father of the Gorgons.

Pontus: Coming from the Greek pantheon, Pontus isn't just a god of the primordial sea; he is the sea itself. He is shown in artwork with a long wavy beard and horns that look like crab claws.

Poseidon: This Greek god of the sea and mariners is usually seen carrying a trident. He was worshiped from around 1600 BCE. He is found in art on sculptures, plaques, and coins, and in literature such as Homer's *Iliad* and *Theogony* by Hesiod. The ruins of the Temple of Poseidon still stand today on a cliff high above the sea in Sounio, Greece; they are a popular tourist destination.

Potamoi: The Potamoi or Potami were the gods of the rivers in ancient Greece. They were most often pictured as carrying an oar, a jug, and a cornucopia.

Tiberinus: Tiberinus is the Roman god of the River Tiber. He is said to have as his consort one of the vestal virgins who perished by drowning. He is said to have an aversion to metal.

Tlaloc: A rain deity from Mexico, Tlaloc is frequently depicted in ancient art pouring water. His worship predates even the Aztecs and was located around Tlaloc Mountain.

Tritons: The Tritons were minor sea gods from the Roman pantheon. They are known to be part of Neptune's royal court.

Varuna: Varuna is the Hindu deity who is the personification of the sky but is also connected to rain, clouds, rivers, oceans, and water itself. In many ways Varuna was considered all-powerful and is described as a wise ruler, an impartial judge, and a leader who was deeply concerned with the well-being of his subjects. He was said to reside in a stone palace located across the sea. People petitioned him for courage and prosperity. As time progressed, he became more directly associated with the ocean and water in general. Images frequently depict him holding a serpent and riding seven swans or even a crocodile.

This list is by no means complete. There are most likely as many gods, goddesses, and deities of water as there are instances of water throughout the world.

Journey Working for the Water Gods and Goddesses

You may wish to do a journey working to help you connect and explore the water energies and entities in this chapter. The following instructions will help you spiritually dive into these mysteries and search for yourself.

Begin by deciding on where you are going to do your working. This could be at home, in a safe indoor space, or outside near a body of water. Whichever you choose, make sure it is somewhere you feel comfortable and will be able to carry out your journey undisturbed.

Next, decide if you will be doing a general working to explore your connection to the water deities or trying to interact with a specific deity. If you are unused to magically working this way, you may think it is easier to start with a general exercise. Then you will need to gather your magical tools to assist you in the experience. I like to include items from each element. You can use a blue candle to represent water of fire, some water incense to represent water of air, actual water either from the site or from some sacred source, and water crystal or some beach sand can be used to stand in for water of earth.

In the beginning it will be much easier if you do this journey work with a friend to help serve as a guide through your journey. Once you become familiar with it, if no one else is available, you can record yourself saying the words and then play it for your journey.

ITEMS:

- blue candle
- glass candleholder
- water
- water incense such as coconut or gardenia
- water crystal such as blue calcite or azurite
- blue cloth

Gather all the items together and set them up on a small blue cloth in front of you. Place a small amount of water in the bottom of the candleholder, then add the candle and light it. You can now also light the incense. Hold the crystal or sand in your nondominant hand (if you are right-handed, this will be your left hand, and vice versa). Next, place a drop of the water on the back of your neck and both of your feet.

Get ready to have your guide say these words:

It will be best to close your eyes to help with this journey. You are going to travel deep into a watery realm, a land of great magic and mystery, where much truth and insight will be revealed.

Know that you are protected, and I will guide you on your journey. The journey you are undertaking will lead you down to another level. Whatever is happening up on this level will not affect you unless you are seriously needed, and in that case, you will be able to return quickly and effortlessly.

Start by imagining a staircase. It can be whatever staircase you like—stone, wood; see it clearly in your mind.

Approach the staircase. You are at the top. You are going to step down from the twentieth step to the nineteenth, then down to the eighteenth, the seventeenth, the sixteenth, moving down deeper to the fifteenth, the fourteenth, the thirteenth, going lower and lower, down to the twelfth, the eleventh, the tenth, down to the ninth, the eighth, deeper down to the seventh, the sixth, the fifth, further down to the fourth, the third, down to the second, then you are at the first, then down to the bottom. At the bottom there is a door. See it. Reach out and slowly touch the door. Say aloud what it looks like. Describe the door. How big is it? What does the doorknob look like? (pause so they can answer these questions; give them as much time as they need)

Reach out and turn the doorknob, open the door and walk through. What do you see? (give them time to answer)

Are you inside or outside? If you are inside, try to find the door to the outside and walk through it. (again, give them time to do this)

Are you outside now? (wait until they answer yes)

What do you see there? Is there water nearby? (give them time to answer)

If so, walk towards the water. If not, still yourself and listen to all the sounds surrounding you. Do you hear water nearby? Do you see any animals or plants that make their home in water? (give them time to answer)

If so, walk purposefully in that direction. If not, walk around slowly until you determine which way you need to travel to find water. Look in all directions—water may be behind you or somewhere you did not think to look. Be patient and trust your instincts. When you find the water, take the time to fully explore the site. What do you see there? (give them time to answer)

What are the colors? What are the sounds? Is there anyone else there that you can see? If so, and only if you feel comfortable, begin to approach them. If you feel comfortable, ask them their name and tell them yours. If you receive a response, repeat it aloud.

If you do not see anyone, take a deep breath, and, with your eyes still closed, look down in your journey at your hands. This will help you orient yourself in the space. Remember if at any time you feel uncomfortable, you are always free to return to the door where you entered and return back up to this space with me. Would you like to continue? (give them time to answer; if they say they would like to return, proceed to the "return journey" directions below)

If you are ready, take a few steps in whichever direction you are called and look around again. What do you see? (give them time to answer)

If there is someone there, and you feel comfortable approaching them, move forward and respectfully introduce yourself. Is there a response? What is it?

Ask if there is any information for you. Ask if there is anything they would like you to know.

Thank them for their time, and when you are ready, you will begin to return to the door through which you traveled to get here. Are you ready? (give them time to answer)

RETURN JOURNEY

See yourself walking towards the door you traveled through to get here. Travel slowly and purposefully. Take note of what you see on your return journey. When you get to the door, open it if necessary and walk through. You will see the same staircase you traveled down. This time you are going to start on the first step. Step up, returning to this level of existence. Go up the second step, then the third. Go up to the fourth step. Keep navigating upward to the fifth step, the sixth, the seventh. Moving up to the eighth and then the ninth step. Feel yourself coming back to this realm. Up to the tenth, the eleventh, the twelfth, the thirteenth step. Climb upward to the fourteenth, the fifteenth, the sixteenth; keep going. Up to the seventeenth, the eighteenth, the nineteenth, and then lastly the twentieth. You are now back in this space with me. When you feel comfortable, open your eyes.

You can now begin to think about what you learned on your journey. It may help to take notes or to otherwise record the experience in a journal or Book of Shadows.

Water gods and goddesses are plentiful. When dealing with orishas, lwas, and African traditional religions, my best advice is always to follow traditional routes and obtain guidance and even possibly initiation from a qualified teacher. Everyone's spiritual path is unique to them, and a teacher will help you to navigate the specific twists and turns successfully. Please remember to be respectful of the ancient systems.

Many different cultures feature gods and goddesses that preside over water in all its guises. There are deities that rule over a specific watery place and those such as Mami Wata who represent all forms of water wherever they may be. They each have their own particular likes and ways of honoring to make themselves known. Take the time to explore their worlds respectfully and you will be rewarded.

Chapter 4

SACRED
WATER SITES

When talking about sacred water, it is absolutely necessary to discuss some of these elemental sites throughout the world. Many are World Heritage sites that are protected for the beauty, majesty, and importance they hold. If you are fortunate enough to have the opportunity to visit these sites in person, I highly recommend it. It will give you a direct connection that will allow you to access the blessings of water in a truly divine way. Even if you are unable to make a pilgrimage to one or more of these sites, please consider honoring the sacred water in your own way in your community. This will help to strengthen your personal power by reinforcing your connections to the spirits of place.

Sacred Water Sites Around the Globe

Bath: The sacred water in Bath, England, has been a sight of pilgrimage and healing for over a thousand years. The use of the hot springs dates back to Neolithic times. They were utilized by the early inhabitants of the British Isles and later the Romans.

The main spring in the area expels around 250,000 gallons of water at a warm 120 degrees Fahrenheit. It is here that ancient Romans and Brits sought to commune with the goddesses and the dead. The water was viewed as a powerful portal to the otherworldly. It was also a site of early settlements. The first shrine there was dedicated to the goddess Sulis.

With the arrival of the Romans, she quickly became associated with their goddess Minerva. In addition to the head of the statue of Sulis Minerva discussed earlier, the temple also had a giant shrine with panels depicting Bacchus, Jupiter, and Hercules. The spring there was most certainly a place for offerings, and over 12,000 Roman coins have been recovered from the site. Of particular interest, over 130 small tablets have been found there on which were written curses, most along the lines of begging Sulis Minerva to punish those who had wronged them. The temples and sacred sites there seem to have fallen into disuse around the fourth or fifth century CE, possibly because of flooding. A Christian monastery was later built on the site around the seventh century. The city itself, including the baths and the remains of the temple to Sulis Minerva, are now protected as a UNESCO World Heritage site attracting approximately 300,000 visitors a year.

Bayou St. John: The bayou is known as a site of powerful magic in Southern Conjure and Hoodoo. Bayou St. John is undeniably the most well-known bayou in Louisiana, if not the world. In the 1700s it was a four-mile-long waterway beginning approximately two miles north of the Mississippi River, winding through the swamp, and connecting to Lake Ponchartrain. It was used by the indigenous people of the area at the time and later became a shipping channel for a brief time. What it is most well-known for, however, is the Voodoo. There are many reports of the legendary Voodoo Queen Marie Laveau performing rites and rituals there. It is here that she is said to have performed some of her sacred St. John's Eve blessings. These are still continued there today where crowds gather on the holiday to receive their blessing at the water.

Boyne River: This river is located next to the passage tombs at Newgrange in Ireland—these gravesites are even older than the pyramids in Egypt. They line up exactly with the sun on the winter solstice, showing us some of the magic and power of the ancient people who lived in the area. The river flows all around these tombs, and during a visit you will most likely cross them, seeing their power and majesty.

Brighid's Well: The Celtic goddess Brighid was a deity who ruled over both fire and water. Over time she has become blended with the Christian St. Brigid. There are hundreds of wells in the UK and Ireland that are considered sacred to this manifestation of the divine feminine. The wells are said to be sites of miraculous healing and blessings.

Chalice Well: Great Britain contains many sacred wells, but one of the most popular is definitely the Chalice Well in Glastonbury. It has long held magical significance but also is said to be the sight where the cup from the Last Supper was washed (or buried, depending on the retelling), causing the waters to become equated with the blood of Christ. Over the years it has become known as a sacred sanctuary that draws numerous visitors each year.

Ganges River: The Ganges River is one of the most sacred water sites in the world. It flows over 1,500 miles from the Himalayas before opening into the Indian Ocean. In the Hindu tradition, it is known to represent the goddess Mother Ganges, known as Ganga Ma in Hindi. For devotees, the river is a source of purification that will wash away their troubles. It is also known to help the dead achieve moksha, a spiritual enlightenment that transcends the cycle of rebirth. Cremations are carried out on the banks of the river. Like many sacred waters around the globe, water from the Ganges River is available for sale online if you care to include this in your spells and workings.

Unfortunately, what has been such a sacred sight is also polluted. Used by millions of people along its journey, it has become a source of toxicity. At the time I write this there have been efforts to clean it, but they remain underfunded.

Guangsheng Temple: Located in Hongtong, Linfen, Shanxi, China, this site houses one of the last remaining water god temples in China. Dedicated to water god Ming Ying King and his eleven attendants, it is decorated with frescoes depicting people praying for rain.

Ibo Landing: The tale of the flying Ibo people has survived for generations. It has been told among African Americans almost since they arrived as an enslaved people. The story is one of resistance and tells of how slaves left in droves, walking into the water and then flying back to Africa. These myths relate not only to supernatural power, but also to the choice of suicide rather than to submit to oppression and slavery. The actual Ibo or Igbo Landing is located in Dunbar Creek, Georgia. It is here in 1803 that a group of Igbo slaves came off the slave ship and marched, singing, to their deaths in the creek. Some reports say just over a dozen bodies were recovered of the approximately eighty slaves who went missing, lending credence to the possibility of escape, either magically or practically. The story is retold in the works of Black writers such as Paule Marshall, Toni Morrison, Jamaica Kincaid, and others. Locals claim that you can still hear the cries and feel the presence of these slaves at the creek. Many consider this act the first real Freedom March on American soil, despite the unfortunate end.

Jin Ancestral Temple: This sacred site dates back to the eleventh century BCE and is located in Shanxi, China, about sixteen miles southwest of Taiyuan, at the base of Xuanweng Mountain at the Jin Springs. The largest building at the site is Sage Mother Hall, which is dedicated to the spirit of the springs there. There are also several other water-related buildings at the site, including an octagonal pool and the Never-Aging Spring. The hot spring continues to bubble up despite all kinds of weather.

Jordan River: The Jordan River, located on the border between Syria and Lebanon, has been considered sacred for thousands of years. There is archaeological evidence that the site was the location of a temple dedicated to the Greek deity Pan from around the third century BCE that lasted almost 700 years. The sanctuary there is located in Golan Heights and encompasses a huge natural cave sitting above a ravine, from which flows one of the tributaries of the Jordan River. There is also a manmade cave that bears the inscription "Cave of Pan and the Nymphs." As time went on, the site began to take on significance in Christianity, the river being named as the place where Jesus Christ was baptized by John the Baptist. It is here that it is believed the Holy Spirit transformed into a dove and appeared. There is evidence it has been visited by thousands of pilgrims a year, even during medieval times. Even today it is considered one of the top holy sites in Christianity. People continue to make pilgrimages there as part of their visit to the Holy Land, both bathing in and drinking the sacred waters.

Lake Lhamo Latso: This lake, situated southeast of Lhasa, is considered the holiest lake in Tibet. It is also called Oracle Lake, and starting with the second Dalai Lama in 1509, it has been a place for these holy individuals to receive visions and information. The site is located at the end of a narrow valley strewn with prayer flags. It also contains a throne where the Dalai Lama sits when in attendance. It isn't just these holy individuals who make the trip, however; several people also make pilgrimages to the area each year, where after fasting and prayer they hope to receive visions of the future themselves.

Lake Manasarovar: This lake located in Tibet is considered sacred to followers of Buddhism, Hinduism, Jainism, and Bön (the indigenous Tibetan folk religion). Almost everything about the place is magical. It is one of the largest freshwater lakes in the world, but the surrounding land is almost like a desert. One of my closest friends just made the pilgrimage there this year and described the experience as truly incredible. Bathing in the water there is said to assist with entry into paradise. Visitors walk around the lake clockwise, stopping at sacred points along the way for bathing and prayers.

Lake Mashapang: This lake in Connecticut, now commonly called Gardner Lake, has its own mermaid legend. It goes a little something like this: the land was once dry and the people were wasteful, ruled by a queen who did not have the intelligence to listen to her advisers. One particular woman, referred to as a prophetess, urged the people to make a change. They did not listen, and the Great Spirit flooded the land. Except for the prophetess, all the residents were killed, and all that remained was the lake where the community once stood. There are reports of fishermen and others on the lake hearing mysterious music.

Lake Pontchartrain: This Louisiana lake covers approximately 630 square miles. It features the world's longest bridge, the Causeway, which connects New Orleans to the other side of the water. Lake Pontchartrain was said to be a ritual sight for Voodoo Queen Marie Laveau. There she performed not-so-secret ceremonies that were reported on in the newspapers and magazines of the time. It is even said she nearly drowned in the lake in the 1880s. Anyone visiting the area can see its power and majesty.

Lake Waiau: This lake is located 13,020 feet above sea level on the summit of Mauna Kea on the island of Hawaii. Locals have historically considered this spot a sacred site and the residence of the snow goddess Waiau. Many make a trip to the lake to witness the magical reflection of the moon on its water. For many years this heart-shaped lake, sitting on a bed of lava, was considered bottomless. It is now known to be roughly ten feet deep.

Loch Ness: Loch Ness is the stuff of Scottish legend. It is home to the infamous Scottish beast "Nessie," who has become an international legend. The loch is actually the largest body of fresh water in Great Britain, traversing almost twenty-three miles, with a depth of about 800 feet. The tales of the beast that is said to live there are even seen on Pict carvings on the standing stones there that date to AD 500. Even Christian history is intertwined with the loch, for it is said that St. Columba traveled to the area and confronted the "monster" with the power of God. Christian reports say it was never seen again, but the local news tells a different story.

Lourdes: This sacred site in France is mainly seen as a place of pilgrimage for Christians in search of healing. The holy well is one of the most popular in the world, with over six million visitors each year. Since 1858 it has been the site of at least sixty-nine miracles or cures verified by the Catholic Church. It is said that the Holy Virgin appeared eighteen times here to Bernadette Soubirous, and it was then the miracles began. It has been the subject of many films, the most famous being *The Song of Bernadette* (1943), starring Jennifer Jones. Over the years the site has become very commercialized, with many comparing it to Disneyland. For those who want to experience the water without making the pilgrimage, this water is readily available through online sources.

Madron Well: This healing well is found in Cornwall, England. Tradition dictates that you must face the sun when receiving blessings from here. The site is also known for healing, and it is customary for children to be dipped in the water three times in an effort to cure them of all sickness and disease.

Mississippi River: The Mississippi has always been a sight of magic. The final stop on its winding journey is the city of New

Orleans. The river was considered a sacred place to the generations of Voodoo queens who have graced the crescent city. Marie Laveau was said to have held ceremonies there, and even today Voodoo priestess Miriam Chamani from the New Orleans Voodoo Spiritual Temple has been known to perform rites and leave offerings there.

Niagara Falls: Every time I visit Niagara Falls, I am truly impressed by its sheer size and magic. Depending on which way you approach it, what you may see is a fairly normal-looking river with no clue what waits just down the way. It was considered a sacred site by the indigenous people of the area. Today it is still one of the most popular tourist destinations in the world.

Nile River: The longest river in the world is the Nile. It flows northward over 4,100 miles, draining out into the Mediterranean Sea. It passes through parts of Tanzania, Burundi, Rwanda, the Democratic Republic of the Congo, Kenya, Uganda, South Sudan, Ethiopia, Sudan, and Egypt. The ancient Egyptians settled around the river in approximately 5500 BCE, and they believed the river was a gift from the gods. Osiris was the Egyptian god of the dead, and it is his death that was associated symbolically with the flooding and rising of the river. This flooding was a vital process responsible for fertilizing the surrounding areas. In the area, tombs were traditionally located on the west side of the river because that is where the sun set every day.

Ojo Caliente: These hot springs are located in New Mexico approximately fifty miles north of Santa Fe. Ojo Caliente was considered sacred to the indigenous Zuni people, who utilized the water in dance rituals to help bring rain and success to the crops. The springs were also prized by many other local tribes, and it has been considered a powerful site for healing and rejuvenation for thousands of years.

Osun River: The Osun River in Nigeria is seen as the home of the orisha Osun. It is surrounded by the Osun Sacred Grove, on the outskirts of the city of Osogbo, which has been designated a UNESCO World Heritage site. Each year the area is home to the Osun festival during July and August that celebrates her and her sacred river of the same name. The land is also home to sacred palaces and worship sites along the river.

Pittsburgh Rivers: Sacred sites are what you make of them, and while many people don't necessarily think of Pittsburgh as a place for sacred water, magical practitioners in the area talk about how the city has its own unique energy because it is founded on three rivers. These rivers are the Allegheny, Monongahela, and Ohio. The rivers meet at a place locals refer to as "the point," where offerings and sacred ceremonies often take place.

Phat Man Dee is a pan-spiritual Jew with Pagan leanings. She works as a jazz vocalist, bandleader, and vocal instructor. She hails from Pittsburgh, PA, where two rivers, the Monongahela and Allegheny, meet to form the great Ohio River. A fourth river flows underground, and it is from that subterranean river that all jazz in the region flows. Pittsburgh native and performer Phat Man Dee wrote the following poem about the magical waters there.

Magical Waters

Dampness seeps into the cracks of the world
Carries spirit from within without
Bogged down forgotten pasts even still inform the future
Carry messages from long ago
And those who float on the surface believe
    they've created them anew

But spirit knows that water remembers all
Falls down, washes back, spins around both
    clockwise and widdershins
Seasons pass, years fade into forgotten memories
Which wash upon the banks with every tide and
    nourish the future generations in muddy glory

Water is life. Mni Wiconi.

Phat Man Dee

• • • •

Pyhänkasteenputous Waterfall: This famous seventeen-meter-high waterfall in Finland has been considered a sacred site for generations and is still one of the most popular tourist sites in the area. The name roughly means "initiation to the sacred" and was traditionally used as a place for making offerings to ensure a successful hunt; it was later transformed by Christians into a site of baptism. This process began when Lutheran minister Esaias Fellman Mansveti performed a mass conversion of the local Sami people in 1648. In the summertime the falls are bathed in sunlight twenty-four hours a day.

Queen Nanny's Cauldron: Queen Nanny of Jamaica is remembered as both a warrior and a queen. Queen Nanny was said to have escaped her own cruel captors and, along with her brothers, founded a free settlement for people of color in the Blue Mountains of Jamaica. From 1728–1740, there Queen Nanny led the group who would later be referred to as the Windward Maroons. It is said that under Nanny's fierce command they managed to free almost a thousand slaves. She used her military skill along with her Obeah talents to successfully complete her campaigns. One of her sacred sights is said to be Nanny Falls in Portland, Jamaica. It is said the water here has great healing powers and was visited by Queen Nanny and her warriors to fortify before battle. Today people take pilgrimages to the area and are able to experience the magical waters for themselves.

She is remembered as a powerful leader and a true force to be reckoned with. There are many reports of Nanny's life. Some recount that she was a slave; some say she may even have had slaves of her own. It is irrefutable, however, that she was a hero of Jamaica who very likely practiced a traditional form of

African-derived religion known as Obeah. Most of history has preferred to forget her connection to African healing methods and magic.

Rhine Valley: This site joined the UNESCO World Heritage list in 2002. It is said to be the domain of Lorelie, the watery siren of legend who was discussed earlier in this book. The mythical creatures of the water known as nixies are also thought to reside there, and on nice days legend says you can see them on the side of the river combing their long blond hair.

Snoqualmie Falls: This sacred waterfall in Washington State is visited by over a million people each year. While the site is probably best known for being featured in the opening credits of the popular cult television show *Twin Peaks*, it is actually a sacred site that has been honored by the indigenous people in the area for thousands of years. For the Snoqualmie people, the site was even featured in their creation story. Legend says that this is the place where chaos in the world was transformed into order. The mist from the falls is said to deliver prayers directly up to the Creator Spirit. The site has also been a place of ceremonial burial and honoring for the indigenous people there.

Urubamba River: The Urubamba River and the nearby heritage site of Machu Picchu have been long considered sacred to the people there. Located close to the river is Tambomachay, which is referred to by some as the Bath of the Inca, recalling the famous UK site. It is said to be a place where you can ritually clean both your body and mind. All of these sites have recently become popular tourist sites for spiritual pilgrimages.

Whanganui River: The indigenous Maori people of New Zealand have an ancestral river they have honored for over 800 years; it is called the Whanganui River. This is the longest navigable river in the country. According to the Maori, their spirit guardians, called taniwha, inhabit this river. On March 20, 2017, the New Zealand parliament recognized into law what the Maori had been insisting all along: the river is a living being. It was therefore granted the same rights, powers, duties, and liabilities of a human individual. The hope is that this will give it some rights and protection from the pollution and degradation it has suffered since the arrival of European settlers in the 1800s.

Local Sacred Sites

This list of sacred water sites is by no means complete; please do what you can to find sacred water sites in your own area and honor them accordingly.

While part of the spiritual experience is always just getting to the actual site, there are some things you can do to help your magic and make your trip more fruitful.

- Consider bringing your ritual tools with you to the site. When you get there, you can then use the water to cleanse and bless these things. Be respectful always, and if your tools are covered with unsavory materials, consider taking some of the water, placing it in a bucket, and using that to wash your items. After you're done, you can then dispose of the water far away from the source.

- Bring a container to collect a small amount of the water you find there. You will then be able to bring it home and use it whenever needed. Please be sure to be respectful, observe local customs and laws, and always leave an offering for the things you are taking.

• Perform a personal blessing ritual at the site. Being at the edge of sacred water gives you a unique opportunity to cleanse yourself and others at the site. Pay special attention to blessing your hands so that everything you touch will be influenced by the power of that water; do the same with your feet and head.

• Research the traditional songs and prayers associated with the site and the divinities that may reside there. Be ready to perform or recite them at the site. The water contained in these sites is ancient, and finding out how it was honored in the past will help you to access its sacred energy and power.

• • • •

The Mystical Waters of Niagara

The following is a guest contribution from Witchdoctor Utu about sacred spaces and rites. Witchdoctor Utu is the author of *Conjuring Harriet 'Mama Moses' Tubman and the Spirits of the Underground Railroad*, founder of the Dragon Ritual Drummers, Niagara Voodoo Shrine, and member of the New Orleans Voodoo Spiritual Temple. Utu has been presenting and performing at Pagan and Conjure events in both Canada and the United States actively since the year 2000.

WATER HAS ALWAYS been part of my life. I was born on an island in Scotland, immigrated in childhood to grow up on the shoreline of Lake Ontario in Toronto, and as a twenty-year-old moved to the Niagara Peninsula. The peninsula is surround by two Great Lakes and the mighty Niagara River that connects them. Niagara

Falls is actually three different waterfalls: the Horseshoe Falls, the American Falls, and the Bridal Veil Falls, which are composed of Lake Erie pouring into Lake Ontario, which then runs out into the Atlantic Ocean via the St. Lawrence Seaway.

It is hard to separate Niagara Falls from either of the lakes it connects to; it's one big sacred dance in eternal motion, continually changing the landscape and dominating the local weather of several surrounding regions. In order to fully understand Niagara's sacred mysteries, we have to look at the largest waterfall in North America as "the doorway."

The word *niagara* comes from the indigenous people that once inhabited the region who were the Onguiaahra, which simultaneously was the name of their waterfall, which meant "the strait" as well as "thundering waters." The waterfalls and its caves were the homes to mythical giant horned serpents, deities of wind, thunder, and lightning. They were also the dwellings of larger-than-life anthropomorphic sorcerers and man-eating stone giants. Niagara Falls is a cataract, a chasm better described as a temple, and a unique mix of sacred blessings and magic, as well as a circus of the macabre to this day. The waters of Niagara Falls are truly waters of natural chaos and primordial power.

When people think of Niagara Falls today, many probably think of its title as the honeymoon capitol of the world, and indeed tourism certainly promotes that and has for over one hundred years. Any waterfall and especially one the size of Niagara produces positive energy in the form of negative ions in the air, hence the renowned mystical and healing qualities that exist in its always-present mist reaching to the sky. The mist itself is deified as "The Maid of the Mist," where an Onguiaahra maiden manifests as an apparition, mesmerizing people for hundreds of years while blessing newlyweds.

Who was this maiden of the mist in life? A sacrifice, according to indigenous lore; whether willing or chosen, she was one of the humans that was in archaic times—long before the Europeans came to the region—offered to the deities of the falls in a canoe to help stop a plague. This ritual was carried out every year after, with the canoe eventually filled with fruit and flowers sent over the falls as symbolic sacrifice. That's Niagara Falls for you: a balance between life and death, comedy and tragedy, celebrated constantly.

The mist of Niagara Falls can change a person's spiritual energy—just by being at the brink of the falls or even close to them, it is a current that runs through the area. When it comes to currents, it was no other than Nicola Tesla who came to the falls and recognized its unique attributes and qualities on more than one level. Tesla is responsible for developing the technology to harness its power through hydroelectricity, and his likeness is immortalized alongside Native American and First Nation legends as well as Victorian-era daredevils in statuary and plaques as he joins Niagara's ever-growing pantheon.

One of the less-focused aspects of Niagara Falls is its subtle but tangible feeling of melancholy from the sheer amount of death and tragedy that routinely take place there. Niagara Falls shares a dubious mantle as a place where sometimes hundreds of people in mere years will choose to end their lives at the falls. Continuing the legacy started with the maiden of the mist, some pilgrimage from across the globe to do so. This adds to its macabre history along with the humans that have and continue to challenge its might in daredevil stunts, trying to conqueror it in barrels and other contraptions, as well as tightropes, to name a few, with not all being victorious.

Niagara Falls is essentially a power point on the globe, a ley line of immense energy as "the strait." It was one of the locations for gathering during the Harmonic Convergence in 1987, with the falls being chosen as a place of power alongside Stonehenge, the Pyramids, Mount Fuji, and Mount Shasta.

Niagara's waters, whether it be the head or mouth of its river or its two joining lakes, also have a water serpent cryptid, which to some is a still-manifesting aspect of its giant horned serpent once venerated by the ancient inhabitants. This horned serpent had many names, depending on the indigenous nation that inhabited Niagara Falls over the ages. To some it was benevolent and helped humans when in need, while to others it was an entity of evil that hated humans and tried to poison its waters and drag people down to their deaths.

In many ways, Niagara Falls defines the many complexities of a sacred waterway and what the water element is: mystical, primal, beautiful, terrifying, indiscriminate, generous, fertile. It gives, takes, and nurtures life, and it houses deities, spirits, and mysteries. To me, however, despite its many layers of legacy and spiritual mystery from the indigenous to the foreign, there is one aspect that truly resonates, and that is "the doorway," the strait. One of the most overlooked aspects of Niagara's unique tapestry of sacred water mysteries is one that continued its legacy as a door—a doorway to freedom. That freedom came to those who fully felt and lived that mystery as they took their final steps towards self-emancipation on the Underground Railroad.

The Niagara River is the very "River Jordan" that is hidden among coded African American Spirituals, with the biblical "Promised Land" and "Canaan" being Canada on the other side of the river from the United States. This was the route made famous by Harriet Tubman, who in her guise as Mama Moses brought many to freedom across the old Niagara River suspension bridge, bringing her people to the Promised Land of Canaan. In many ways, this makes the river an embodiment of holy water. (The Detroit River was also a crossing point and final waterway to freedom on a different route of the Underground Railroad, and so it also shares the mysteries of the River Jordan.)

Rivers and creeks continue to serve as a place of cleansing, washing away what we no longer need in order to be reborn, and so it's no surprise that rivers and creeks are places of baptisms and spiritual passage rites. In the traditions I have been taught and schooled in, living waters are the most effective to use. Rivers and creeks are unique as their currents, even if they are gentle, still carry away burdens and things we can wash away. Rivers or creeks are also places to scatter spell contents and magic that is no longer needed. They can help reverse magic that is in effect against us because the current and the life force of the water carry it away and subdue whatever we scatter or place in the river. If water is used to contain rods from nuclear fission, then it can do the same to spellwork that we may need to offer to it.

Niagara Falls certainly serves many spiritual needs. The indigenous legacy varies from Nation to Nation on either side of the white man's border. Its power is harnessed to provide hydroelectricity to much of the Eastern Seaboard of North America. It is a global tourism destination to celebrate love and consummation of marriage. It's a New Age location that attracts spiritual tourists and seekers looking to commune with its positive energy, albeit just underneath there lies a palpable level of darkness and death lost on many. There are countless paranormal hot spots attributed to a host of reasons, and it was the place of immense and brutal battles fought during the War of 1812, being as it was an official border even back then. But throughout it is a "strait," a place of movement between two Great Lakes traveling towards the Atlantic Ocean, a doorway between two countries and to many spirit worlds.

Like most rivers, it was settled because of commerce, whether by the indigenous peoples of the region or the colonizers that came long after. There is a reason so many cities, mills, and settlements are built upon the banks of rivers, and in this modern age that reason escapes folks. Regardless of where we live, as spiritual practitioners and witches, we can harness even the gentlest of rivers, like Tesla did with Niagara, only do so on a magical level. As a reader and spiritual adviser, I oftentimes suggest various formulas for people to help with their prosperity, business ventures, and the like, and quite often these people, like myself, live along rivers, creeks, and lakes. This is a variation of magic that is adaptable to one's own creativity in order to personalize it, and at times I suggest it during spiritual consultations as a simple way to harness the living life force of any local creek, river, or lake to enhance one's power of place.

Witchdoctor Utu

• • • •

Honoring the Local Waterway

Whatever waterway exists near you, whether a mighty river, large lake, creek, or series of ponds, chances are your settlement was built there because of them and what they offered. Back in pre-colonial times in North America, that would have included hunting and fishing. But the colonizers had other ideas and built mills, docks, and factories, causing immense destruction and pollution. Regardless, the local waterways are living life forces, each with their own personality and identity.

You can stand at the edge of any local waterway and honor it and call its name, whether it's an older indigenous name or the one that was placed on it long after. That is its name you can say aloud—say its name and introduce yourself.

Tell the water you cherish its life force and all of its fish, crustaceans, insects, birds, and animals that live along and with it.

Offer your sympathy towards its almost certain state of some level of pollution. As a spiritual worker, this is an important thing, to let the water know we empathize and cherish all of its life.

You can bring some fresh water with you that you can pour into it as a libation with your love and gratitude. You can also offer a few flowers, either purchased or picked along the way, again as a gift to the water.

You could also add a few pennies at the edge of the river to pay for its favor; a few won't hurt, and the symbolic gesture can go a long way magically in the reciprocity you seek.

Tell the water you honor it. In these modern times, the industries that were once built along the waters are almost scarce, now a ghostlike energy of a time long ago but still able to be harnessed.

Ask for its energy of motion and abundance towards your needs. As well, you could offer small bits of bread or foods that the fish or birds would enjoy to again offer sustenance and gratitude towards its life.

When you feel you have communed and communicated with the water, gather some in a small container to bring home and anoint your threshold or even the inside of your dwelling. You could create a wash with other ingredients, depending on the purpose at hand. By doing this, you sprinkle the now blessed and honored waters of your region, empowered and awakened to bring forward water's power of prosperity for you and your work.

Include the occasional or regular visit to your local river, creek, lake, or ponds, bond with it, call its name, and commune with its life force and what lives among it. In this way you will better harness the power of place where you live and carry on the tradition and witch's work of conjuring the element of water before you. Prosperity and motion towards your magic will surely increase as you work intimately alongside your waterway, as witches have done throughout time.

Sacred water is all around us. Each drop contains its own magic. Some are healing; some provide keys to the past and maybe even the future. The waters can be used to bless or even to use as a passageway to other realms. Exploring the sacred sites both near and far will help you get in touch with all the glorious manifestations of water throughout the planet. This should be done with mindfulness and respect. Consider not only what you can take away from the space, but what you bring to it as well.

PART
2
❧

WORKING WITH THE ELEMENT OF WATER

Chapter 5

THE ELEMENT OF WATER
IN MAGIC

Water manifests as an element in ourselves and also in our surroundings. It works in conjunction with the other elements of fire, air, and earth in a myriad of ways. Water combined with fire creates steam. Water combined with air creates vapor and humidity. Water combined with earth creates mud. Each of these has its own unique healing and transformational properties. Steam baths are a traditional healing process throughout many parts of the world, while vapor has been known as a medical treatment for disorders concerning breathing. Mud, too, is something that is a time-honored healing technique in the form of mud baths and treatments, which people pay dearly for in spas.

In magic, water is often marked by the following glyph, which is symbolic of the cup, chalice, or other container that would hold water: ▽.

CHAPTER 5

Honoring the Element

There are many simple things you can do both physically and spirituality to honor the element of water in and around you.

- *Drink water.* I know it sounds very basic, but few people actually get the recommended amount of water a day. Whenever I am feeling a bit challenged during my busy days and nights, I do a quick self-check and find that I'm often making things more difficult for myself by forgetting to drink enough water.

- *Take a bath.* Taking a bath is an easy way to immerse yourself in the power and majesty of this element without even leaving your home. Consider using some of the ritual baths featured in this book or coming up with one of your own.

- *Swim.* Floating, swimming, diving, or otherwise immersing yourself in water as it manifests in nature is a direct connection to this divine element.

- ***Place water on your altar or shrine, especially remembering to give water to your ancestors.*** It is interesting to me that many different spiritual traditions employ this belief. In the African traditional religion known as Ifá, often offerings consist simply of a glass of water. There is even a proverb that says "Those who offer water will have a time of rest." Remembering to offer water to your ancestors and on other shrines you may have in your home will assure you are granted much-needed peace inside.

Water reminds us to keep moving forward—however, when assigned a direction in Witchcraft, water is usually associated with the west. It is represented by the colors blue and sometimes gray. In that direction cauldrons, mirrors, chalices, and actual water are used as tools of the element. In some traditions this is also the direction for the ancestors, the dead, and otherworldly beings. Because of this connection with those that have gone before, many Wiccan circles start their rituals with chants and calls to this element.

Water Altars and Shrines

Water altars and shrines can be general or specifically created to honor a particular god, goddess, or water entity. An altar is set up as a temporary space for a specific magical working, while a shrine is created to be a permanent place to worship and focus your spiritual energy. Think carefully about where your altar or shrine will be located, as it should be placed somewhere you can interact with it undisturbed from external influences. If there is not a permanent place for your altar or shrine, consider making a smaller, more portable one. This can be done in a small box or tin and then be closed and put away when not in use.

Customarily a general water altar or shrine would feature a blue altar cloth, which is representative of the element. I like to use a natural fabric like cotton or silk. If you are making one that is specific to a god or goddess, you may wish to incorporate fabric that uses some common motifs or symbols. For example, if you are setting up a space to honor a deity of the sea, there are fabrics that contain images of waves or sea birds that you can utilize. Whatever cloth you use will be the base of your altar or shrine. Next, you will begin to assemble your actual elemental items.

Clearly, the most important feature you include will be the actual water. This can be contained in a dish, bowl, chalice, bottle, or whatever else you wish. Choose your materials carefully; obviously a wood bowl will react differently than a glass or metal one. This vessel will hold your actual water. Many witches choose to include spring water, sacred water from a blessed river or well, ocean water, or any other type they find significant to them. You may also wish to consider adding a fountain. Several years ago, when I was going through a difficult time dealing with my emotions of grief and anger, I purchased a large fountain of malachite, turquoise, slate, and chrysocolla. It helped me to both explore and accept some of these feelings, and it certainly made the whole space much more pleasant. Falling water—as found in both waterfalls and fountains—is known to produce negative ions, which are said to provide both vitality and energy.

In order for your space to operate most effectively, you will need to also have the other elements represented. You can add a blue candle sitting in a candleholder filled with water, and you can even use candles that have water-themed herbs and oils added to the wax. If you are adding these items after the candle has already been created, please do so in moderation, as too much may cause the candle to smoke excessively or even become overly inflamed. You can use an incense blend dedicated to a water goddess or god, or just use some of these water herbs burned on a piece of charcoal to represent the air element. The element of earth can be present in this space in the form of sand or dirt from the shoreline. Alternatively, you could use a watery crystal such as turquoise or moonstone on the shrine. You are limited only by the extent of your imagination. I know one outdoor event space that features a water shrine made out of an upcycled rowboat painted in swirls of blue and decorated with starfish, shells, and other items from the sea.

Another valuable feature to consider adding is a water elemental figure or statue. This could be of the water goddess or god you are focusing on, a water-loving animal like dolphins or ducks, a mythic creature like a mermaid or a selkie, or just about anything else water related. When creating spaces like these, it is best to be guided both by your spiritual teachers and also your intuition. There have been instances when items literally fell into place right on or near my shrine as I was walking past. Alternatively, there have been other times when things have had a difficult time being included, and I found them being knocked over or misplaced. I received a good piece of advice many years ago when a friend told me to mark the exact location of your statues, as sometimes they may seem to move and shift without any outside help. There are many beautiful commercial statues and artwork available out there, or feel free to create your own piece of artwork. Just make sure it is something that will be able to command and focus your attention as you interact with it in your sacred space.

Please do your best to clean and maintain your sacred space on a regular basis. To achieve the best results, it should be treated with the utmost care and respect. It is always a good idea to use some of your magical waters as part of the regular cleaning and blessing of the space.

Types of Water

Water is water—or is it? There is spring water, holy water, rainwater, river water, storm water, glacier water, ocean water, waterfall water, pond water, well water, and many more. It can be solid, liquid, or gas, changing its character frequently. Each one of these specific waters will create their own unique magical energy.

Note: No water is to be gathered without leaving some type of offering. Magic operates on a system of exchange, and you must give something in order to achieve something. When gathering waters I often will leave offerings of coins, spirits, food, flowers, or the like. It is best to gather your sacred water into a glass jar or bottle; be sure to label it with the type of water, the date, the moon phase, and the weather conditions (storm, snow, or whatever is appropriate).

Dew Water: While very difficult to collect, dew water is great to use in love magic or as an offering to the fey, or Faery world.

Glacier Water: Water from a glacier can be used to provide your magic with clarity and a connection to the ancients.

Hurricane Water: This is obviously a very specific type of storm water. It is one of extreme strength and power. Hurricanes bring quick and sudden change. The water gathered at this time can be used for change, too, in addition to justice and protection. In the religion of La Regla Lucumi, the hurricane is the domain of the orisha Oya.

Lake Water: This type of water is said to bring calm, peace, and joy. It is also useful for workings concerning self-reflection and self-assessment.

Ocean Water: Ocean water, like the other waters, takes on the local energy of the site. The Atlantic Ocean will have a very different vibration than the Pacific and other oceans. Obviously, it will be easiest to obtain water from a source close to you. Ocean water is a common offering in the religion of La Regla Lucumi for the orisha Yemaya.

Pond Water: This water is useful for creating opportunities, self-discovery, and relaxation.

Rainwater: This water is one of the best to use for your magic. Many witches believe that May rainwater is the best because when gathered at this time, it takes on the character of Beltane. This is a time when the earth is said to celebrate fertility, newness, rebirth, and success. This water can be utilized for blessings, cleansings, prosperity, love workings, and just about every other kind of magic.

Snow Water: Snow can represent purity and change, and the water from it can be used in magic for the same purpose. The Yule season is a wonderful time to collect snow as it will be full of the magical energy of that time of year.

Spring Water: Spring water is heavily influenced by the surrounding spirit of place. It will take on the unique character of where the spring is located, be it the mountains, the forest, or elsewhere. As a rule, however, spring water is associated with newness and bounty. There are many sacred springs such as the ones in Bath, Lourdes, and elsewhere throughout the globe.

Storm Water: Storm water hurls itself at us from the heavens with a powerful force. Many times it is accompanied by thunder, lightning, and fierce winds. Traditional Witchcraft tells us that this water can be used to strengthen spells and workings. It can also be used for protection, motivation, and rebirth. On a darker note, some individuals use this for hexing, cursing, and revenge work.

Swamp Water: Swamp water has a character all its own. Often mixed with algae, silt, and even mud, it can be fetid and funky. Magical practitioners often use this type of water for workings dealing with binding, banishing, hexes, curses, and magic involving revenge.

Urban Water: Urban water, like all waters, has a unique energy influenced by its environment, but that doesn't mean it's not magical. Traveling throughout the streets and tunnels of a city, urban water has a journey that is serpentine and purposeful. If you live in an urban environment, this water carries the energy of your spirit of place. Very often it comes from a major river or body of water near the city. The tap water in Paris is made up in part from the Seine River; the same is true for London, with a percentage of the tap water coming from the Thames. The unique character of these rivers will then lend their energetic influence to your spells and workings. Because urban tap water passes by rich and poor residents of the city, you can use it in magic both for success and prosperity and also for curses and hexes (while I don't advocate for these types of spells, I certainly understand why individuals use them).

Waterfall Water: Water from a waterfall is rejuvenating. It creates a newness and an energy that is unlike any other.

Well Water: Well water is useful in magic for granting wishes, healing, and connection to otherworldly beings.

Sacred water holds a special place in many different cultures. In Southern Conjure water is a vehicle for travel and transformation. In Buddhism water is one of the four major elements, and it is used for cleansing, purification, and sacred offerings. It represents clarity and the flow of existence.

Water and Chakras

Water is associated with the sacral chakra, the second of the seven main chakras. This chakra is called Svadhisthana and is located in the lower belly. It is associated with your relationship with yourself and others; it is a seat of creativity and joy. *Svadhisthana* translates to "one's own abode" or "the dwelling within." Sexuality and pleasure are also governed by this chakra. The color of this chakra is orange, and meditating with candles of this color may help to activate and heal this chakra. The mantra for this chakra is the word *vam*. Chanting it is said to help one heal from a poor self-image or difficulties in relationships and sexual encounters.

Water and Feng Shui

Feng shui is the Chinese system of geomancy, which governs the placement of items to improve energy and success. The very words *feng shui* translate into "wind and water." Water is one of the five sacred elements in feng shui. It will help to attract both freedom and flow into your space. Water is also said to govern status, wealth, and prosperity. Obviously you can represent water in your own environment by using actual water in the form of a fountain or bottle of water, by using the color blue, having fish, or displaying an artistic representation of water or marine animals. However, feng shui is all about balance, so if there are imbalances in your life, make sure water isn't dominating that area in your home. The system of Kanyu is what informs feng shui. Kanyu is the name of the geomantic system that recognizes the natural energy of the environment. Kanyu recognizes placement of water not just inside your home but in the external surrounds as well. I have had several feng shui classes and consultations over the years, and I highly recommend learning from a professional if you want to seriously incorporate these practices in your own home.

Water in Astrology

The element of water is connected to the astrological water signs of Cancer, Scorpio, and Pisces. These people are said to possess a dreamy, fluid, and watery nature that can cause them to be led by their deep emotions and feelings. As sun rulers, the influence dates of each sign are approximately as follows:

- Cancer: June 21–July 21
- Scorpio: October 21–November 21
- Pisces: February 21–March 21

Each one of the signs is associated with a different animal and a planetary ruler and has its own glyph. Cancer is considered the sign of the crab and is ruled by the planet Venus. Scorpio is often symbolized as the scorpion, lobster, or crawfish, and it is ruled by Mars. Finally, Pisces is the sign of the fish and is ruled by the planet Neptune; it is also often associated with the moon. In astrological writing, these signs are symbolized by the following glyphs:

- Cancer: ♋
- Scorpio: ♏
- Pisces: ♓

The different associations reflect the different characteristics of each water sign. Here are the keywords associated to each sign:

- Cancer: loving, cautious, protective, nurturing, moody
- Scorpio: passionate, magnetic, forceful, secretive, jealous
- Pisces: compassionate, spiritual, intuitive, idealistic, escapist

Water in Tarot

When people think about elemental water magic, they will often think about tarot and the suit of cups. Cups are the tarot suit traditionally aligned with water. Most tarot scholars will tell you that cups are associated primarily with the emotions and love in particular. If one looks at the physical characteristics of this suit manifesting in the page, knight, queen, and king, these cards often represent people who have fairer skin and blond hair with blue or green eyes. In addition to the individual's physical characteristics, these cards can simply represent the astrological sign of the person in question. For example, the Queen of Cups may represent a mature, fair-haired woman or a mature woman whose natal sun is in a water sign.

Ace of Cups

Like all the tarot suits, the cups begin with the ace. Numbered one, the Ace of Cups most often shows a single cup or chalice. This has been said to represent the Holy Grail. The grail, the most famous cup in Christianity, is said to have been the cup Jesus drank from at the Last Supper. It also features prominently in the legend of King Arthur. The cup is said to hold the keys to eternal youth and happiness. The Ace of Cups in many ways symbolizes this bountiful happiness and joy. The water it contains has been likened to the contents of the witch's cauldron and the Fountain of Youth. The cup is said to hold boundless potential, just like the element of water itself.[34]

In addition to the cups cards, there are a few trumps (major arcana cards) that are associated with water. If one looks at the classic Rider-Waite deck, it is filled with the traditional symbols for the cards. These are echoed throughout many other decks and tarot interpretations. The element of water is a significant feature most notably in the Death, Temperance, Star, Moon, and Judgement cards.

Death

The Death card is numbered 13 and is certainly one of the most powerful cards in the deck. As a child I watched a lot of bad television; this card would always appear in scenes with a stereotypical psychic, and tragedy was sure to follow. In reality the Death card doesn't necessarily mean actual death but instead complete transformation. The water seen in this card isn't the prominent feature; it is featured in the distance. This makes it present but not an immediate issue. Many decks see this card as a movement away from difficulty, a change on every level. I have heard this card referred to as unwilling or unwelcome change. This is an interesting way of looking at it. Many of us fear change, even though it is the one constant in the universe. Ultimately all things die or are transformed, and, for better or worse, everyone must make their

---

34   Nichols, *Jung and Tarot*, 1–7.

peace with it. Change cannot be stopped, and neither can the tides, or the currents of water here on earth.

Temperance

In the Rider-Waite deck, the Temperance card immediately follows the Death card and is numbered 14. It has water featured both in the form of a pond or pool literally front and center and being poured back and forth from the two chalices. Temperance is about balance, like the water that pours back and forth between the two cups. In the Thoth deck, Crowley talks about dissolving a pearl in wine as part of the meditative energy for this card. Sometimes this card is given the alternate name of Art.

The Star

The Star card, in my opinion, is one of the most beautiful, both in its imagery and its meaning. It is said to represent destiny, hope, knowledge, vision, healing, calm, transcendence, transformation, and inspiration. The card can be seen as a guiding light in the universe that shows you the way to your dreams.

The Moon

In Tarot decks the Moon represents things that are unseen and hidden. Like water itself, it frequently represents deep emotions and feelings. Traditional imagery for this card usually features two dogs or jackals and a crab, crawfish, or lobster crawling out of the water. Some have theorized that the image of a dog contrasted with that of a wolf or a jackal are representative of both the tame and wild sides of our unconscious nature. Here one sees that all three watery zodiac signs are present in this card: the crab (Cancer), the crawfish or lobster (Scorpio), and the moon (Pisces).

In some decks this card features water falling from the sky. The water could be seen as rain or tears; some see it as the pull of the moon lifting water up out of the seas. The moon is known to control the tides and has a supremely powerful effect on water.

Judgement

Judgement is one of the last cards in the deck. It is numbered 20, and the idea of finality is highlighted here. It traditionally features an image of the angel Gabriel blowing his trumpet. He is said to help with communication and protection. The water in the card is calm and placid. It is known to represent return and renewal as well as regeneration on a deep level. There is a change here, too, but this time it is a complete and total new beginning based on your past deeds and works.

• • • •

In a Word, Water

The following essay is from Alyson G. Eggleston, PhD, a linguist and writer living in Charleston, SC, with her two feline familiars. Fascinated with human language, much of her work focuses on the effects of language on our thinking and problem-solving abilities. She is also passionate about language as a tool of access and enjoys equipping young folks with the tools they need for success and discernment.

WATER: LIFE, MOTION, energy—if these are the concepts summoned to mind when you hear or say what was probably among the first words you spoke in your mother tongue, you're right on track with the historical and linguistic roots of this precious, mysterious substance. Forms of the word from Early Old English (AD 600–1066) provide scholars with clues of its origins. Used mostly in compound phrases, the concept was rendered as uaeter or uuaeter[35] until sound changes happening due to language contact and conflict in the southeast of what is now England resulted in the more familiar-looking Middle English forms: water and vater.

But this is only the story as it comes to us through the Germanic branch of the Indo-European family tree, a web of related languages that connects languages spoken in Europe, India, and parts of Central Asia to one single prehistoric parent language, Proto-Indo-European. Linguists and philologists like Sir William Jones and Franz Bopp[36] were among the first voices to draw cohesive evidence that languages as disparate in place and time as Sanskrit, Hittite, Latin, Persian, German, Greek, and Irish are all, in fact, related. Here's where it gets interesting: words that identify universal concepts that all cultures need or use are often linguists' first targets when we investigate possible family connections between spoken languages[37]—and "water" fits that bill! A universal need and resource, "water" is among the Swadesh 100, a list of words American linguist Morris Swadesh curated as universal concepts during his fieldwork with North American indigenous languages and their speakers.

35   "water, n." *OED Online*, Oxford University Press, December 2019, www.oed.com/view/Entry/226109. Accessed 6 January 2020.

36   B. W. Fortson, *Indo-European Language and Culture: An Introduction*. Wiley, 2011. Web. Blackwell Textbooks in Linguistics.

37   M. Swadesh, "Lexicostatistic Dating of Prehistoric Ethnic Contacts," *Proceedings American Philosophical Society 96*, (1952), 452–463.

English "water" shares the same pan-Indo-European base as the Hittite *uiten-* and *uitar*,[38] forming a family line that goes back at least 3,500 years in time and connects the northwestern fringe of Europe with the language of an Anatolian empire. Without detailing the sound change patterns over time, the Sanskrit *udan*, the Greek ὕδωρ, the Old Church Slavonic *vodan*, and the Irish *uisce* are all daughters of the reconstructed Proto-Indo-European mother form *wódr*.[39] The Latin *unda*, meaning "wave," is another related descendant form, but this one encodes the idea of water in motion. You may more easily recognize the unda root in a word like "undulate."

Just as speakers can emphasize the motion and direction of water, they often encode references to water as an alcoholic spirit, and the Oxford English Dictionary reports this etymon pattern as widespread among the European languages. *Uisce*, from which we derive "whiskey," *vodan*, root of "vodka," and Latin *aqua vitae,* or "water of life," are all Indo-European word forms for distilled alcohols.

So remember, when you purse your lips together as you ask for that thirst-quenching substance, your mouth is producing a sound pattern that has changed very little over thousands of years. Other Indo-European language speakers were making similar echoes as you are now, uttering the same word: water.

Alyson G. Eggleston

• • • •

---

38   T. Olander, P. Widmer, and G. Keydana, "Indo-European Accent and Ablaut," Museum Tusculanum Press, University of Copenhagen, 2013. Web. Copenhagen Studies in Indo-European.

39   When linguists propose reconstructed proto-forms of words and word-roots, the asterisk is used to distinguish the form from historically attested and written forms.

The element of water is vital for all living things. Magically it helps us heal, get in touch with our emotions and the emotions of others, travel, and transform. By fully exploring and understanding the element of water and all it is associated with, its true power and ultimate potential can be unlocked.

Chapter 6

WATER HERBS AND BOTANICALS

Water botanicals and water plants get their association in a number of different ways. First, there are herbs that are associated with the moon, or the watery zodiac signs of Cancer, Pisces, and Scorpio. Then there are herbs and plants that represent this element because they grow and thrive in water or very watery conditions and environments. Finally, some people consider certain botanicals to be water plants because they bear particularly juicy fruit or sap. The following list is extensive but by no means exhaustive. Feel free to add your own favorite water herbs into your rotation whenever possible.

Note: Some individuals can experience a negative reaction when ingesting these ingredients or even using them on their skin. Please consult with a medical professional and use extreme care when dealing with unfamiliar ingredients.

Aloe (*Aloe barbadensis*): The humble aloe vera plant has become a standard in modern healing. Here in the US it is available to use both topically and as a drink or supplement (however, it is toxic at certain levels, so consume with caution). It is composed of 96 percent water, so there is no surprise it is on our list of water plants. There is evidence that aloe has been used as a medicinal herb for over 2,000 years. Placing a live aloe plant in your home is said to protect your space from accidents and other mishaps. In certain areas of Africa, it is hung near the doors and windows to keep away the evil eye. Sacred to Venus and Aphrodite, it can be used as an offering to them on your altar or shrine. Magically it can also be used in workings for love and beauty.

Apple (*Malus domestica*): Apples are a traditional offering for Hel, Hecate, Lilith, Santa Muerte, and Changó. You can use the fruit of the apple, the flower, or even the bark in your magic spells and workings. It is influenced by the planets Venus and Jupiter, and you can use it in connection with these. I have always seen apples as inherently magical. In the Bible they are seen as representing knowledge. If you slice one open horizontally, it will reveal a five-pointed star, an elemental symbol highly prized in Witchcraft. The powerful fruit is used in magic for love, romance, passion, divination, psychic connection, and healing.

Ash (*Fraxinus americana*): Ash is one of the most magical trees around. It has long been a chosen wood for spiritual tools and creations such as wands and brooms. Ash is said to grant protection, strength, power, psychic dreams, prosperity, and luck. Ash trees themselves are said to attract lightning, so don't take shelter under one in a storm. The spiral-shaped buds of the tree are believed to mimic the cosmic spiral of life. It was a sacred tree for both the ancient Egyptians and Druids. Early Norse mythology tells us that this tree was known as Yggdrasil, the tree of life connecting the nine worlds.

Balm of Gilead (*Cammiphora opobalsamum* or *Populus candicans*): According to biblical lore, the Queen of Sheba gifted this plant to King Solomon. Balm of Gilead in either floral or oil form is a regular ingredient in Hoodoo spells. The song "There Is a Balm in Gilead" is a traditional African American spiritual that dates back to the 1800s. The origins of the song are not totally clear, but in many different versions it says this balm can be used to cure one's soul. Magically the plant can be used not only to heal and in matters of love, but also to consecrate, bless, and purify.

Bay (*Laurus nobilis*): Bay leaf is used very often in kitchen witchery and Hoodoo. You can use the leaves to write the name of your lover and carry it in your pocket; alternatively, you can use the leaves to write the names of your haters and burn the leaves to remove their influence from your life. Bay is a common houseplant, and growing a bay tree in your home is said to protect it from thieves and accidents. It is considered sacred to the orishas Obatala and Babaluaiye.

Buckthorn (*Rhamnus cathartica*): There are several different varieties of this small tree, which is native to Asia, Europe, North America, and Northern Africa. Many people view it as a nuisance plant, as it can be invasive. Magically it is a plant used for protection workings. It is said to repel negativity, demons, poisons, and the evil eye. Traditionally branches were hung from doors and windows to accomplish this purpose. It is also used in workings to remove blockages and grant your deepest wishes.

Burdock (*Arctium lappa*): This plant is also known as bat weed, gobo, beggar's buttons, and love leaves. Carrying burdock root has long been said to be a source of power and strength. It also has several medicinal properties and is widely used by herbalists even today. Consequently, it is also used in magic for healing as well as cleansing and protection.

Calamus (*Acorus calamus*): Among the common names for calamus are sweet flag, sweet grass, sweet rush, myrtle grass, and gladden. It loves to grow near water, and that is the reason for its association with this element. It can be used in magic for controlling and dominance, as well as for protection, luck, healing, and strength. This is used as an offering for the orishas Oshún and Ochosi.

Catnip (*Nepeta cataria*): Anyone who knows cats knows that catnip can be a recreational drug for their pets. Consequently, it is sacred to Bast, as well as Freya and Aphrodite. It is primarily used as an herb for love. It is used as an attractant and works in spells to bring love and passion to your bed. It can be added to washes, baths, and oil formulas to capitalize on these effects.

Chamomile, German (*Matricaria recutita*): This plant is associated with fairy magic. It is known to bring about relaxation, calm, peaceful sleep, luck, protection, and gentle love.

Coconut (*Cocos nucifera*): Both the oil and the flesh of coconut are common ingredients in many kitchens. There are many magical uses for the coconut too. It can be used to bring purification, cleansing, and blessings. In La Regla Lucumi, coconut is very often an ingredient in ritual washes, and people are often advised to bathe in the water of a freshly cracked coconut. Coconut is said to be sacred to the orishas Yemaya and Eleggua.

Coltsfoot (*Tussilago farfara*): A member of the daisy family, this plant is found growing naturally in Europe and Asia. The medicinal properties of this herb have been lauded for thousands of years, and it is used to treat coughs and colds. Magically coltsfoot is used to grace altars and shrines during the holidays of Imbolc and Beltane. You may wish to use coltsfoot in your rituals and spells for peace, love, calm, and connection to the psychic realms.

Comfrey (*Symphytum* spp.): A member of the borage family, there are over thirty-five different plants that are commonly called comfrey. The most popular use of this herb is in magic for traveling and protection. For decades I have made sure to include a small piece in my luggage to make sure it doesn't get lost. In addition to this, the herb is also helpful for protection and grounding work. Some people can have a reaction when their skin touches comfrey, so please be careful the first time you touch the fresh version of this plant.

Cucumber (*Cucumis sativus*): This common vegetable has been cultivated for over 3,000 years. Being composed of approximately 96 percent water, it is no wonder it finds itself on our list of water plants. Magically it is said to help with love, lust, and healing. Slices of cucumber placed on the eyes are said to help improve psychic visions.

Cypress (*Cupressus sempervirens*): Cypress is one of those plants that thrives in water. Often it is found thriving in swamps and watery areas. It is said to bring blessings of healing, protection, wealth, and success. It can be utilized as a sacred offering for Hecate, Hera, Athena, Aphrodite, Astarte, Oya, Yemaya, and Nana Buruku.

Elder or Elderberry (*Sambucus* spp.): There are over twenty-five different varieties of this plant, but black elder is the most prevalent here in the USA. Like many of the water plants on this list, it is known to grow best in watery conditions, near the edge of a lake or stream. This plant has long been used for healing. Commercially prepared cough syrups and tonics from elderberry flowers or juice are widely available. They are said to help with fevers, flu, coughs, and also boost the immune system.

The ancient Druids were said to hold this tree in high regard, and it is one of the plants used in their Ogham system of divination. Elder is depicted there by five lines and the letter "R." There it is said to represent the cycle of life, the ever-present interplay between life and death, this world and the next. However, it isn't just the British Isles that utilized this magical plant. It is linked to early Germanic, Scandinavian, and even Christian concepts. Some call it the Judas tree and say that this is where the rogue apostle chose to hang himself.

There are many folk beliefs and superstitions surrounding this plant. One legend says that certain powerful witches possess the ability to shapeshift into these plants to avoid being seen. The sap that runs when the branches are cut is said to be their blood. Because of this it is very unlucky to cut down this tree, and elaborate permissions are asked beforehand. Wands made from elder are said to have the power to banish negativity, and it is a great wood for crafting your ritual tools. People also craft beads and instruments from the wood to help with protection and also for connecting to the Faery realm.

The Druids assigned this tree to the thirteenth month, the time between November and December that happens to include Yule. Any late berries that still cling to the plant can be used to make a powerful elixir or wine, which when drunk during Yule is said to bring prophecies and messages from the otherworld. Large quantities of elder are toxic, so please refrain from trying this on your own. St. John's Eve, observed on June 24, is also an auspicious time to gather these berries and use in spells and workings to protect you from misfortune and harm and grant you great blessings. An equal-armed cross can be made of the wood and tied with red cord; this can then be hung from doors and windows to prevent harm from coming to the house. Elder is also a plant used for honoring and communicating with the dead. In many countries small shoots of elder were planted on graves to help the dead find their way to a blessed afterlife.

Elder is considered an appropriate offering for the goddesses Hel, Venus, and Hilde. Elder is a valuable ingredient in magical spells and rituals for intuition, prosperity, protection, healing, wisdom, judgment, rebirth, transformation, removal of jinxes and hexes, banishing, and exorcism.

Eucalyptus (*Eucalyptus globulus*): This is one of those healing herbs that has found its way into common practice. You can even buy cough drops with this magical ingredient. In addition to its healing abilities, eucalyptus is known to promote concentration, focus, clarity, balance, divination, and psychic ability.

You can also use it in magical workings to help with calming anxiety and panic attacks. It is considered sacred to the orishas Obatala and Babaluaiye.

Gardenia (*Gardenia jasminoides*): These white flowers are said to symbolize love, devotion, purity, and spiritual connection. The Victorian language of flowers says they represent a secret love affair. If you were surprised by one of these on your doorstep, your secret admirer had come calling. Because of their connection to love magic, they are often used in wedding bouquets and arrangements. You can use oil of gardenia in your baths, floor washes, and ritual oils, or just place the actual flowers on your altar or shrine. It is considered sacred to Isis, Hecate, Aphrodite, Kuan Yin, and Obatala. There are lots of uses for this water elemental plant and luckily it can be grown easily at home, either indoors or out.

Heather (*Calluna vulgaris*): This plant, also called ling, or Scotch heather, is found growing in Europe, Asia, Greenland, and North America. Traditionally it has been used to make brooms, brushes, and baskets, and it was even used as a building material to create small buildings in the Scottish Highland. Its botanical name, *Calluna*, comes from the Greek word *kalluno*, which means "to cleanse." Consequently, small bundles of heather can be tied together to make brooms or scourges for using with your ritual waters and washes. The famous author Robert Louis Stevenson writes about this delightful flower in his ode *Heather Ale*:

> From the bonnie bells of heather,
> They brewed a drink long-syne,

Was sweeter far than honey,
Was stronger far than wine.[40]

Clearly people have valued the benefits of this delightful flower for centuries. It can be used in your magic for luck, success, self-control, protection, purification, adoration, passion, and the granting of wishes. Heather is said to be especially prized by the fairies and can be given as an offering to them. Some even believe it opens the doorways between our world and theirs. It is also considered sacred to Isis, Cybele, Venus, and Eleggua. In Ireland incense and offerings of heather are used to bring about communication with those who have passed on. The white variety is considered particularly auspicious.

Hyacinth (*Hyacinthus orientalis*): One of the most delightfully fragrant spring flowers is the hyacinth. I would bathe in its delicious scent every day if I could. They bloom in an absolutely gorgeous array of colors—blue, purple, pink, white, and yellow. Magically they can be helpful with joy, happiness, calm, peace of mind, freedom from oppression, and removal of negativity. It is sacred to the orisha Yemaya.

Iris (*Iris* spp.): There are approximately 300 different species of iris. Irises are thought to be ruled by the moon and are therefore very useful for divination and other psychic work. They are said to bring faith, courage, and great wisdom. Often the root of the plant is used, which is called orris root. When growing irises in your garden, remember they thrive in damp soil, especially when in full bloom. In the Greek pantheon, Iris was a goddess who ruled over the rainbows and the seas. She functioned as a

---

40   Stevenson, *Ballads*, 67–68.

messenger between worlds, riding the rainbow to deliver the important words and information. Because of this, magically irises are still used for communication, especially when sending messages of love. In addition, irises are used for love, romance, protection, psychic power, and divination. They are given in offering to Erzulie Freda Dahomey and also to Hera, Aphrodite, and Venus. (*See also* orris root)

Irish Moss (*Chondrus crispus*): Not a moss but rather an algae or seaweed, Irish moss is one of the most watery plants around. Historically it has been used in brewing and is common to all lands that border the Atlantic Ocean. The magical uses for this plant include gambling luck, protection, travel safety, and success in business. It is used as an offering for Brighid, Aphrodite, and Maman Brigitte.

Ivy (*Hedera* spp.): Ivy is a common garden plant throughout most parts of the world. While there are several different species that fall under this name, English ivy, classified as *Hedera helix*, is one of the most popular. Ivy is known to be toxic, so do not ingest this plant. Sacred to Ariadne, Arianrhod, Artemis, Bacchus, Dionysis, and Osiris, this plant is firmly rooted in magic.

A favorite of poets and artists, in 1862 Christina Rossetti wrote the following about ivy:

> Oh roses for the flush of youth,
> And laurel for the perfect prime;
> But pick an ivy branch for me
> Grown old before my time.[41]

---

41   Gifford, *The Wisdom of Trees*, 109.

Ivy is easy to grow both indoors and outside in most areas. Planting it around your home is said to help keep it safe on every level. It is said that if ivy thrives on your property, you will be successful. In addition to success, Ivy is also said to be useful in magic for fidelity, relationships, fertility, protection, and health. Because of its ability to thrive in many diverse environments, it is said to teach us the value of perseverance. It can also be used to increase the speed and effectiveness of your spells.

Jasmine (*Jasminum* spp.): There are approximately 200 different species of plant that are known by the name jasmine. Its name is Persian in origin and roughly translates to "gifts from god." The plant is useful in magic for divination, psychic connection, joy, happiness, healing, love, and abundance. It is said to help stimulate and heal the heart chakra. Jasmine is considered sacred to Aine, Aphrodite, Bast, Diana, Hecate, Ishtar, Venus, and Orunla. It is said to be ruled by the moon and is sometimes given the poetic name "moonlight on the grove."

Lemon (*Citrus limonum*): Lemons are sacred to Juno, Luna, and Yemaya. Folk magic tells us to place a slice of lemon beneath each chair at the dinner table to keep the peace among guests. Either the juice, the leaves, or the fruit of this plant can be used. In your magic spells and recipes, lemon can help to impart blessings of love, romance, joy, peace, protection, and purification.

Lemon Balm (*Melissa officinalis*): This delightful herb has been in use since ancient times. Sacred to Artemis and Yemaya, there are many magical uses for this plant. You can add it to spells and rituals for strength, calm, wisdom, love, passion, and joy.

Licorice (*Glycyrrhiza glabra*): Licorice root is an ingredient in many medicines and confectioneries. It is sometimes even used to flavor tobacco. There are prohibitions for people who are pregnant, nursing, or suffering from heart problems. As always, consult with a physician before ingesting. It is used in spells for commanding, compelling, and controlling; however, these workings often have problematic results, so proceed with caution. Magically it is also used for workings for passion, love, and working with the dead. The plant can be found growing wild in Greece, Spain, Italy, Iraq, Syria, Russia, and even China. Fortunately, you can also grow it at home. Be sure to soak the seeds thoroughly before planting as this will help them sprout quicker and more effectively.

Lilac (*Syringa vulgaris*): Growing up, lilac was one of the few flowers that regularly found a place in our home. It was the favorite of my grandmother, who, despite her red-headed temper, was often calmed by the delightful scent. The fragrant blooms are also beloved by many types of butterfly, as well as the orishas Oshún and Yemaya and the lwa of the cemetery, Maman Brigitte. It is said to have the ability to drive away ghosts from your property, as well as bring protection and positive energy. Lilac can also be useful for divination and accessing knowledge from past lives.

Lily (*Lilium* spp.): There are daylilies, water lilies, and calla lilies, just to name a few. Each one manifests with its own unique type of magic. Daylilies are said to help with birth and parenting; they are also useful when trying to forget your troubles and cares. Lilies in general are associated with the Virgin Mary as well as Hera, Juno, Venus, Obatala, and Oshún. You can use them in your magic spells and rituals to grant passion, fertility, love, birth, progress, development, hope, faith, renewal, and remembrance. They are also helpful in rituals when communicating with the dead.

Lobelia (*Lobelia erinus* or *Lobelia inflata*): The tiny blossoms of this flower are said to be especially loved by fairies. Lobelia is used in workings for love, romance, protection, cleansing, and weather magic. Throwing it in the direction of a coming storm can make it change its path.

Lotus (*Nelumbo nucifera*): Lotus is used in workings for divination, meditation, healing, and protection. It is also used as an offering to Yemaya, the orisha of the ocean, and Oshún, the orisha of the river, as well as the goddess Isis.

Nettle (*Urtica dioica*): Nettle, also called burn hazel, burn weed, or devil's plaything, is a plant that is known for its sting. It is used for hex breaking, jinx removal, protection, and exorcism.

Orris Root (*Iris germanica* and *Iris pallida*): Queen Elizabeth root is another name for this popular ingredient in spells and workings. Mainly it is used for love, romance, heart healing, and protection. You may also use it in conjunction with the heart chakra. It is a traditional offering for the orishas Eleggua and Orunla.

Passionflower (*Passiflora* spp.): Just as the name implies, these flowers are used to bring passion, love, and sensual pleasure. There are a whole host of plants in this classification that bear the name. They are said to remove negativity and illness while attuning your energy to higher vibrations and psychic knowledge. Passionflower is also used as an offering to the orisha Changó.

Peach (*Prunus persica*): Most kitchen witches are familiar with the delicious peach. Archaeological evidence tells us that peaches have been eaten since around 2000 BCE. They are particularly prized in Chinese culture, where they are said to grant vitality. The blossoms, wood, and fruit are all used in magic. Peach wood is used for both wands and dowsing rods, while eating peaches is said to create an atmosphere of love. They are considered sacred to Aphrodite, Freya, Hathor, Venus, and Oshún. Magically they are used for romance, passion, sensual pursuits, fertility, longevity, and the granting of desires.

Periwinkle (*Catharanthus roseus*): Sorcerer's violet is another name for this delicate treasure that has long been a favorite of witches. Periwinkle can grant peace, calm, harmony, money, success, love, passion, and psychic knowledge. Folklore says that parents who have lost children should plant it on their child's grave to help them heal and keep the good memories alive.

Plumeria (*Plumeria rubra*): Plumeria is my favorite scent. It has been used by the perfume industry since the seventeenth century. Also called frangipani, it is said to help stimulate the crown chakra and open up receptivity to other worlds. Magically it can open one up to sensuality, attract love, improve self-confidence, and instill inner peace.

Poppy Seed (*Papaveraceae* spp.): Poppies are used for pleasure, success, divination, healing, and honoring the dead, as well as in spells for invisibility. They are also used in spells for confusion and overcoming addiction. Ironically, poppies are also the main ingredient in the manufacture of addictive drugs like opium and heroin. The flowers and seeds of this delicate beauty are used to honor Hecate, Aphrodite, Hypnos, Demeter, Persephone, Venus, and Nyx.

Pomegranate (*Punica granatum*): Pomegranates are associated with the goddess Persephone and her tale of the underworld. The fruit was made infamous through this story of dark and light. It may feature in other epic adventures as well: certain theorists suggest that the fruit in the garden of Eden was really a pomegranate and not an apple. The fruit is used in magic spells and rituals for fertility, prosperity, abundance, money, protection, divination, knowledge, and wisdom. Some practitioners even use pomegranate juice as a substitute for blood in rituals and formulas. It is held sacred by the goddesses Astarte, Persephone, and Sekhmet.

Rose (*Rosa* spp.): Roses are representative of love in almost every culture. Even nonmagical people use them to symbolize their love for each other and enhance their romantic pursuits. They can be given as an offering to Oshún, Yemaya, Pomba Gira, Adonis, Freya, Hathor, Hecate, Demeter, Isis, Santa Muerte, and many other manifestations of the divine. In addition to love, they can be used in your rituals and spellwork for divination, psychic connection, healing, luck, protection, purification, and more. Both Jewish and Islamic folklore tell of rose's ability to reveal the truth, so you may wish to consider using them for this purpose too.

It takes over two thousand roses to make one gram of rose oil, making it highly prized and quite expensive. As an alternative, I frequently use rose water in my ritual baths and washes. There is even a food-grade option easily obtained from gourmet stores and retailers that can be used for your kitchen witch creations. Even though it isn't thought of as a traditional ingredient, I like to cook with rose whenever possible; I find it imparts a loving harmony to the food and all those who eat it. Rose flowers and petals also make a beautiful addition to your altars and shrines.

Rose of Jericho (*Selaginella lepidophylla* or *Anastatica hierochuntica*): The magic of the rose of Jericho plant is that it comes back to life when placed in water. Also known as resurrection plant, it is good at renewing things that have become dead or stagnant. This could be your finances, business, love, relationships, or health-related issues.

Sage (*Salvia officinalis*): There are over a thousand species of plant referred to as sage. Common sage (*Salvia officinalis*) is the one most often used in cooking. It can also be applied to a variety of magical uses. White sage (*Salvia apiana*) is also used for sacred purposes. Pregnant women and nursing mothers should note that this herb can reduce milk supply.[42] These days sage has become one of the most popular witchy herbs around. Sage is said to be useful when working with the third eye, crown, and sacral chakras. Magically you can use it in spells and workings to remove negativity, banish nightmares, gain clarity, remove ego traps, center yourself in the universe, and attract money. There is almost nothing it can't do. It is sacred to the goddesses Brigid and Hecate, the gods Zeus and Jupiter, and the orishas Obatala and Eleggua.

Sandalwood, White (*Santalum album*): Sandalwood is a wood that is used in magic for protection, purification, psychic con-

---

42   Simpson, "4 Things That Can Decrease Your Milk Supply."

nection, success, joy, and healing. Sandalwood is used through-out the world and has been part of the ritual process in India, China, Tibet, Egypt, and elsewhere. It is considered to be a plant ruled by the moon, so you can use it in your astrological spells for this purpose. Sandalwood is also an appropriate offer-ing for the goddesses Freya, Lilith, and Venus, and also the ori-shas Oya, Changó, and Yemaya. The most popular way to use sandalwood is to burn it as a resin or incense; in fact, the smoke is a common way to purify ritual tools and items in Hindu temples, where it is called chandan. The smoke is also said to aid with meditation and focus and is therefore often added to other blends to improve their potency.

Unfortunately, this is an herb that is threatened, especially Indian sandalwood, which has been overharvested and is facing extinction. Please purchase your magical items mindfully and responsibly.

Spearmint (*Mentha spicata*): In Spanish cultures this is called yerba buena, which translates to "good herb." And a good herb it is, as spearmint is used for protection, fortitude, love, clar-ity, psychic knowledge, healing, and spiritual cleansing. As the name implies, it is a member of the mint family, which gets its name from the fact that the leaves are shaped like tiny spears. There are also many spells that use spearmint for banishing negativity and bad energy. It is offered to Aphrodite, Pluto, Yemaya, Eleggua, and Changó.

Sweet Pea (*Lathyrus odoratus*): This flower was a standard in Vic-torian gardens and is still very popular today. The flowers come in many colors: pink, red, white, violet, or purple. They are native to the Mediterranean but are easily cultivated in other areas. Magically they are used in spells and workings for friendship, love, affection, and removing unwanted defenses. In the language of flowers they were said to mean "goodbye." Sweet pea is a customary offering for the orisha Oshún.

Tansy (*Tanacetum vulgare*): Tansy is a member of the Daisy family that is said to simultaneously repel pests and promote health and healing. Also called fairy buttons or bitter buttons, traditionally tansy was used as a funeral herb and was used in preparations for the dead. Tansy contains a toxic chemical called thujone, so do not eat and please proceed with caution when using it in your magic. Because of its association with death, it is also said to be an herb that fosters immortality and longevity. Tansy is used primarily to keep one safe from sickness and disease, and a smudge made from it was often used to cleanse and protect one's home. Similarly, boughs of the herb were tied to doorways and windows for the same purpose. When planted near your home, it is said to chase away storms and lightning. Tansy is said to be sacred to the Virgin Mary.

Thyme (*Thymus vulgaris*): A common cooking herb, thyme has many magical applications as well. In your spells and rituals it can be used for healing, loyalty, affection, love, romance, courage, divination, psychic power, legal problems, grief, and protection. Thyme has been in use for centuries in many different parts of the world. In ancient Egypt it was used as an herb of the dead and was often included in funeral rites and rituals, while in ancient Rome it was eaten by statesmen and military leaders to prevent poisoning. In Victorian England thyme growing was thought to signify the presence of fairies.

Tonka Beans (*Dipteryx odorata*): These delightful beans are the product of a flowering tree native to Central and South America. The use of tonka beans as a culinary ingredient has seen a recent resurgence. Historically, tonka beans were used as a highly prized ingredient in creating vanilla extract until they were banned in 1954. The beans are toxic, but that has not deterred people from continuing to use them as a nonedible ingredient in their magic spells and potions. A popular Hoodoo item, the lucky beans are used for manifesting your utmost desires and wishes. They are particularly effective when used in spells for love, romance, and partnership.

Valerian (*Valeriana officinalis*): Most often the root of this plant is used, and an alternate name for it is vandal root. It possesses a strong and unique odor that is often a substitute for musk or other animal ingredients in spellwork. Magically it can be useful in work for healing, harmony, strength, sleep, calm, and turning bad situations into good ones. The root is also used as an offering for Aphrodite, Hertha, and Venus.

Vanilla (*Vanilla planifolia*): Like all other orchids, the vanilla plant is ruled by the planet Venus. It is known for possessing the magical properties of beauty, clarity, communication, healing, love, joy, psychic knowledge, empowerment, and energy. Vanilla was prized in ancient Mexican culture and used both as a precious beauty aid and an aphrodisiac. It is considered a sacred offering for Lilith, Hecate, Oshún, and Eleggua.

Violet (*Viola odorata*): Luckily for us, violets grow wild in many parts of the world. There are over 500 different species of this flower, most colored in white, yellow, or the familiar purple.

The tiny treasures are said to grant success in matters of love, lust, simplicity, serenity, peace, and luck. Ancient Greeks are said to have used these flowers to promote peaceful sleep and good dreams. In the language of flowers, their meaning is "faithfulness." They are associated with fairies and children. Violets are edible, so they can make a great addition to your kitchen witch creations.

Willow (*Salix* spp.): Witchcraft and willow trees go hand in hand. Witch's brooms (besoms) are traditionally made from willow branches, and magic wands can be made from the branches as well. Willow trees grow well near water, thriving on the edge of lakes and rivers. The branches are also said to make great dowsing rods, containing the ability to find water and hidden objects. It is one of the plants used in the Celtic Ogham alphabet and is representative of the fifth month. The tree is considered sacred to Artemis, Brighid, Cerridwen, Diana, Hecate, Persephone, Luna, Selena, and Maman Brigitte. Willow is associated with the moon and is said to magically help with psychic dreams, divination, empathy, enchantment, astral travel, grief, and healing. Willow is also known to provide a gentle, calm, loving atmosphere. The active ingredient salicylic acid has long been used in making aspirin, so even traditional medicine recognizes the healing value of this plant.

Ylang-ylang (*Cananga odorata*): Called the "flower of flowers," this powerful plant is known for bringing strong passion, true love, calm, success, foresight, opportunity, joy, and an irresistible quality to your magic. It can be used as an offering for Eleggua and Oshún.

This list is only a beginning. It should be considered a strong foundation to the whole host of herbs and botanicals that you can use in your water magic. Consider including them in your magic garden, leaving them as offerings on your altar or in nature, or incorporating them into your magic spells and formulas.

Chapter 7

WATER CRYSTALS, STONES, AND SHELLS

Water crystals, stones, and shells can make a beautiful addition to your water altar or shrine. They can also be worn as jewelry, used to create a crystal grid, added to a medicine or mojo bag, carried in your pocket, placed under your pillow, or used in any number of other ways to bring their energy and influence into your life. Water crystals will help to impart a grounding or earthy energy to your magic.

Crystals and Stones

Some crystals and stones are associated with water because they used to be in liquid form—amber is an example of this. Other stones get their association with water because of their blue color. Some crystals end up with this connection because they are formed in water. Despite this, not every crystal does well in water and may even be toxic, so please check before you place them in a drink or a bath.

Alexandrite: This crystal is a form of beryl. It is said to help on many levels, bringing joy, creativity, intuition, psychic ability, and help with manifestation of desires. It is one of the hardest gems in existence. Alexandrite is considered very rare; in some cases, it is more expensive than diamonds. I have a very lucky friend who found some of these at an estate sale. They were originally named for the famous Russian prince Alexander II as they were discovered on his birthday in 1830. Carrying this stone is said to attract extreme good luck and a direct connection to the divine.

Amber: Amber is not actually a stone but the hardened form of a plant resin. You can get pieces that have plants or even insects trapped in the resin and subsequently frozen in time. In combination with jet, amber is considered a witch's stone. It is useful in your magic to gain wisdom, healing, longevity, protection, purification, beauty, and love. It can be used when working with your sacral chakra. Many use it as a protective healing charm for children, especially when they are teething (be careful the baby doesn't eat it). Amber is considered sacred to the goddess Freya and the orisha Oshún.

Amethyst: Amethyst is said to help you connect to higher realms and also grant you insight in every situation. Visionary Leonardo da Vinci believed amethyst could strengthen the intelligence. It can also help grant mental clarity, spiritual connections, happiness, romance, self-love, and self-awareness.

Azurite: One look at the vibrant blue crystal known as azurite and you can see its magic. Azurite is named for its deep blue color, which is most likely why many associate it with the element of water. The stone is said to help with intuition, clarity, insight, meditation, calm, peace, emotional healing, and astral travel. Despite its association with water, you should keep this stone away from water as it has a tendency to disintegrate. It can be used in conjunction with the crown, throat, and heart chakras.

Beryl: Beryl is actually a family of stones which include aquamarine, alexandrite, emerald, morganite, bixbite, and others. It has been prized for over 4,000 years as a source of healing, hope, happiness, and relationship harmony. Like many of the water crystals here, it is used to drive off demons and bad spirits.

Blue Calcite: Calcite in all its manifestations is said to help with spiritual, emotional, and physical growth. It can be utilized for creativity, hope, courage, success, vision, and psychic knowledge. Blue calcite can be used when working with both the throat and crown chakras. The stone will help with communication on every level. Place a piece under your pillow or bed to bring prophetic dreams and the ability to remember them. There is also a custom of keeping one in your home or place of work to prevent thieves from taking your property.

Blue Chalcedony: This stone is particularly helpful when meditating. It is said to grant harmony of mind, body, and spirit. Chalcedony is also known to help with communication, remembering past lives, and activating the throat chakra. Some also recommend giving it to children to help with anxiety, fear, and nervousness. The crystal is found in India, Turkey, Brazil, and Madagascar.

Chrysocolla: The most common form of chrysocolla is colored a bright greenish blue, but it also manifests as brown or black. In all its colorful forms, this is a stone of communication on every level. Helping one to speak their truth, it is especially good for healing and stimulating the throat chakra. Use it when working to balance the throat and the heart chakras for clear and loving connection and communication. In the US it is found in Pennsylvania, Utah, New Mexico, and Arizona. Frequently it is found mixed with quartz, malachite, and other crystals.

Coral: Coral is one of the few things on this list that actually comes from the ocean. There are many different types of coral, and each one carries its own special properties. There is red, brown, blue, and black coral.

Emerald: Another member of the beryl family, emerald is a popular stone for jewelry and decoration. It is seen as a special stone for the deities Ceres, Isis, and Vishnu. The Egyptian god Thoth was said to have had emerald tablets that revealed great magical wisdom and mysteries. Emerald is also called the stone of truth, which is said to also bring good luck, psychic visions, and healing from emotional wounds and breakups. Because it is connected to the heart chakra, many view emerald as a stone of love and partnerships. Some even believe that if the stone suddenly changes color, your partner has been unfaithful or dishonest. In many ways this semiprecious gem is about balance, both within yourself and in your relationships with others.

Green Calcite: Green is one of the types of calcite often associated with water. It helps to heal anxiety, nervousness, and mental imbalance. Green calcite is also helpful for ridding one of things that are no longer useful and for overcoming trust issues.

It can be worn to help with healing, but then it must be spiritually cleansed often.

Jade: Jade comes in a whole host of different colors, but green is the one most commonly connected to the water element. Jade is representative of love on every level: divine love, self-love, romantic love, and all the rest. It is associated with the goddess Kwan Yin, a beacon of love and compassion. Jade is also seen as a very lucky stone that brings clarity and insight.

Jet: Jet is prized for its unique ability to completely transform a negative situation. It operates like an energy filter that has both the ability to protect and purify. You can even use jet to clean off and energetically clear other stones.

Lapis Lazuli: Lapis is one of the most popular stones for magic in general and water work specifically. It is used for love, healing, and psychic power and connection.

Moonstone: Moonstone is directly ruled by water and the moon. It is a stone known to grant love, happiness, and joy, and it opens your mind to serendipity and insight. When worn or placed under your pillow, moonstone can bring calm and healing to your unsettled emotions.

Mother-of-Pearl: The stones known as mother-of-pearl are actually created from the lining of pearl oyster and abalone shells. They are prized in many different cultures and have been utilized for thousands of years. Mother-of-pearl items were even unearthed in Egypt's pyramids. In ancient times Romans carried the tiny pearls to ensure success when traveling over water. They are still used today to bring prosperity, focus, purification, protection, and connection to higher realms. Mother-of-pearl is also used for banishing and transmuting negative energy. It is used in jewelry, to make accessories such as buttons, and as inlay in furniture.

Obsidian: This stone is made from molten lava that was cooled so quickly it solidified into a crystal. The most common form is black, but it can also be rainbow-colored or blue, green, brown, or with a silver or gold sheen. Like the element of water, it is known to reveal things that are hidden. Magically it is known to remove negativity, depression, unnecessary blockages, and heal difficult emotions. Obsidian is connected to the zodiac sign Scorpio.

Opal: All opals have a watery nature, but hyalite water opal is particularly associated with this element. The stone is associated with hope, joy, and luck. It is also known as an amplifier for insight and psychic connection.

Pearl: Pearls belong on this list of water stones and crystals more than any other. Pearls, which are in reality stones, grow inside marine mollusks. Growing up, I was taught pearls can mean either good or bad luck. These tiny treasures have been prized for millennia. Pearls have a connection to both water and the moon. They are said to bring their wearer prosperity, luck, and love. Many legends talk about the powers of pearls, and one of the most well-known myths tells us that they are formed from raindrops swallowed up by oysters. Some even believe that they come from the tears of the biblical Eve, who cried as she was forced to leave the Garden of Eden.

Peridot: I always think of peridot's unique color as a curious green. The stone's name comes from the Greek word *peridona*, meaning "abundance." It is also said to be a powerful charm against the evil eye. It has been prized for thousands of years both for its beauty and to bring success, clarity, friendship, love, and protection. Even Emperor Napoleon was said to have gifted jewelry made of this stone to Josephine as an emblem of his undying love and devotion.

River Agate: There are a number of different types of agate, and many are named for the rivers and other bodies of water they are found in. There is Savannah River Fairyland Agate, Lake Superior Agate, Cave Creek Agate, and China Lake Plume Agate, to name just a few. Agate is said to promote harmony, relationships, love, luck, and success.

Riverstone: Geologically this stone is related to limestone. It is plentiful throughout the world and can be found almost anywhere. Riverstone is said to help with luck, success, happiness, and healing difficult emotional states. It is said to facilitate quick and necessary changes in your life. When worn it is said to rejuvenate one's mind and body on a deep level.

Rose Quartz: Rose quartz is a commonly used crystal for accessing both personal and divine love, friendship, and healing. Often referred to as the heart stone, this has been prized as a talisman for love for thousands of years. It is associated with water and can be used to access emotions. Rose quartz can be used as a ritual offering for Freya, Yemaya, Venus, Isis, Hathor, and several other deities. This ancient crystal is prized by many goddesses and is used to contact all aspects of the divine feminine.

Sardonyx: This crystal is found in Russia, India, Brazil, and parts of Asia. It creates an atmosphere of joy, optimism, and courage.

Sodalite: This is another of the blue-colored stones that finds itself associated with water. Sodalite is one of the best stones to use when speaking truth to power. It is said to connect your thoughts with your feelings. It is sometimes mistaken for lapis lazuli, which contains golden flecks and highlights. It isn't just Western culture that values this stone; it is also used in feng shui to represent the element of water, which helps things to move and transform.

Sugilite: This stone was only discovered in 1944 in Japan, but it has quickly become popular for many different reasons. It is a great crystal for unification between the heart and the head. It helps to heal both the heart and the crown chakras, clearing them out and realigning them.

Topaz (Blue): This crystal is said to bring good fortune, intelligence, beauty, healing, self-love, and long life. Some individuals call this the "writer's stone," as it is supposed to remove writer's block and foster creativity. It is said to stimulate both the throat and the third eye chakras.

Tourmaline (Blue): This stone can be found in the USA, Brazil, Sri Lanka, Nigeria, Kenya, and Afghanistan. Tourmaline is one of the best stones to use when trying to transform situations that aren't working. Many people are used to seeing black tourmaline, but it also comes in an amazing blue color. Blue tourmaline, also known as indicolite, helps to elevate one's consciousness, protect, and bless an individual. This form of tourmaline works especially well with throat chakra work. It can be used to become a better communicator both in the spirit world and the mundane one. This stone is good when connecting with spirit lives and past-life recall. It is also said to bring wealth and success and improve memory.

Turquoise: Because of its intense blue color, many people associate turquoise with water. It is, in fact, created by water pushing through deposits of copper and aluminum. Magically turquoise is said to bestow healing, joy, luck, and longevity. Turquoise is highly prized in many different cultures: Native American, Egyptian, and more. The name itself comes from the French and means "Turkish."

Sacred Shells

Any comprehensive book about water magic has to talk about shells. They are like solid manifestations of the water's energy, true gifts from the splendid sea. Many people collect seashells; there are even entire stores dedicated to them. Different shells obviously carry different messages and meanings.

There are numerous ways to incorporate your favorite shells into your magic. Shells can be used directly on your ritual altar or shrine as candleholders, incense burners, offering containers for water, and in many other ways. They can be used on their own or in concert with crystals in a grid, which utilizes the power of sacred geometry. Ritual baths and floor washes are also great ways to use shells in your magic. Be sure to rinse them thoroughly before use.

There are many spells and potions in this book that incorporate shells, but feel free to use your intuition and craft your own as the spirit moves you. Shells can also be a useful addition to your divination practices. In the African traditional religion of Ifá, cowrie shells are used for divination. If you so desire, you can also craft your own set of runes out of seashells. Use ones that are relatively uniform and cleanse them periodically with ocean water for best results. Another useful idea is to make your own divination set using just the shells themselves. After making yourself familiar with their basic properties, place them in a bag; you can then do draws to help find guidance and insight into your particular situation. Really, your own imagination is the only limitation to how you can use these watery treasures in every aspect of your magic.

Clam Shells: Often these shells are used in spells for love, romance, protection, and purification. My grandmother was from New England, and consequently I have spent a lot of time there. The indigenous people of this area highly prize clam shells, or "wampum," as they are often referred as. While history has erroneously taught us that this was used as money, it was instead utilized as jewelry and was created into highly prized beads and decorative charms that were representative of status and power. You can add these to your magic both for offerings to the spirits of the land and to help unlock your own unique powers.

Cockle Shells: The popular phrase "warms the cockles of my heart" gives us a clue that this shell is used for love magic. It also helps in workings for friendship, emotional healing, and harmony.

Conch Shells: Conch shells make magic with their divine sound. Some consider them the earliest musical instruments. Their sound is deep and commanding, echoing the deep power of the depths from whence they came. Their powerful music heralds the start of something seriously special.

I have seen these shells used in the traditions of New Orleans Voodoo and Haitian Vodou. Magically they are said to symbolize good luck, prosperity, fertility, success, birth, weddings, and regeneration. In certain areas they are left on cherished graves, much in the same way as flowers.

The intricate spiral of the conch is said to symbolize infinity. In Buddhism the shell is one of the eight auspicious symbols representing the fame of Buddha's teachings that spread throughout the world. In India the conch also features prominently in epics and religion. It is said to represent power and authority and is used to banish negativity, prevent disaster, and repel poison. There it is used as a musical instrument and also a container for holy water.

Cowrie Shells: In ancient Egypt cowrie shells were prized as great magical tools. Certain cultures believe that their special magic comes from their resemblance to a half-open eye. Other groups see a similarity between the cowrie shell and female genitalia, and consequently they have become symbolic of fertility and success. African traditional religions recognize these blessed shells as the divine tools of Ifá. They are used for both psychic readings and blessings. Cowries attract insight and financial prosperity. They can also be thrown into a moving body of water, such as a stream or ocean, while a wish is being made. Throw the shells, then leave and don't look back.

Limpets: In general limpets are said to grant confidence, courage, and strength to accomplish your goals. Keyhole limpets (*Fissurelildae*) are a family of sea snails that feature a tiny hole in their cone-shaped shells. Like the holey stones discussed before, this hole seems to hold great magic for connection to other worlds and unlocking difficulties and problems you may have.

Nautilus Shells: Because these creatures are always growing, this shell can be used in workings for renewal and growth.

Oyster Shells: Oyster shells are often used in rituals and spells involving the full moon. These could be for romance, love, luck, success, healing, and more. It seems like most of the lore surrounding oysters is similar to that of the pearls they contain.

Sand Dollar: Etched by the Goddess on the top of every sand dollar is a five-pointed star, evoking the witch's pentacle. They are even referred to as witch stones and are used in spells for wisdom, healing, necessary growth, and the release of outmoded ideas and patterns.

Scallop Shells: Scallop shells are good for workings involving movement and travel. In the Bible these shells are associated with St. James and represent the dual nature of humankind. Both the physical and the spiritual are brought to the fore here. St. James was a pilgrim who eventually became the patron saint of Spain. Devotees today still travel the "Camino de Santiago," which translates to the Way of Saint James. They are said to carry a scallop shell to signify their spiritual journey.

Whelk (*Buccinidae*): This shell is used in spells for control and power in a situation. It also helps to grant stability in your life.

Gem Water Recipes

Making gem waters has become all the rage lately. You can even get special bottles designed for just this purpose. You don't necessarily need a special bottle, but you will need some basic information and items to get started. Gem waters aren't complex; they are simply gems in water. By doing this, the water becomes infused with the power and energy of the crystal. This water can then be used for blessings, baths, and washes.

There are many crystals that are *not* to be placed in water, some because they will disintegrate, others because the result will be toxic.

Crystal elixir bottles have become common, and these come in styles where the stones are separated from the water or inserted in it. The bottles that keep the stones completely separate can be useful if you need to use a stone that you are unable to place directly in water. I have even seen straws that have crystals inside them. Feel free to experiment with these, using some of your favorite stones accordingly.

Following is a list of crystals that should not be placed directly in water. This list is by no means exhaustive. Please do your own research and proceed with caution, especially if you are thinking about making waters to consume.

Crystals That Should Not Be Placed In Water

Actinolite	Adamite	Ajoite
Alexandrite	Amazonite	Atacamite
Auricalcite	Azurite	Beryl (including aquamarine, bixbite, emerald, goshenite, morganite)
Black Tourmaline	Boji Stones	Bronchantite
Cavansite	Calcite	Carnelian
Celestite	Chalcantite	Chalcopyrite
Chrysocolla	Cinnabar	Conicalcite
Copper	Covelite	Desert Rose
Dioptase	Dumortierite	Moldavite
Moonstone	Morganite	Opals
Pearls	Pietersite	Emerald
Galena	Garnet (including almandine, hessonite, rhodolite, spessartine, uvarovite)	Gem Silica
Halite	Hematite	Iolite
Kunzite	Labradorite	Lapis Lazuli
Lepidolite	Magnetite	Malachite
Markasite	Mica	Mohawkite

Prehnite	Psiomelan	Pyrite
Realgar	Ruby	Sapphire
Torbenite	Tourmaline	Tremolite
Turquoise	Vanadinite	Wavellite
Selenite	Serpentine	Smithsonite
Sodalite	Spinel	Staurolite
Stibnite	Stilbite	Sugilite
Sulfur	Sunstone	Tanzanite
Tiger Eye	Topaz	Wulfenite
Unakite	Zircon	Zoisite

Crystals and shells are powerful components to add to your magical water workings. Because of their nature, they bring a solidifying earth energy to all that you are doing. As this list shows, there are a wide variety of stones and shells to choose from, each with their own delightful magic and character. Play around with them and consider carrying them in your pocket or even placing them under your pillow so they can bless your dreams.

Chapter 8

WATER ANIMAL GUIDES

Animal guides can appear in dreams, waking visions, or reality to help you learn important spiritual lessons and give you vital messages. They can help us navigate our lives. There are lots of ways to recognize these special beings in our world. It could be that you have always had a special affinity for an animal, and this may be one of your patron animals. It could be that you keep seeing an animal, either in person or represented elsewhere, and this could be pointing you towards it as one of your guides. It is important to remember that these connections cannot be forced but instead appear exactly when the time is right, reminding us of the importance of both patience and respect.

Some people discover their animal guides through journey work or careful observation of events in their life. Some people find their animal guides through divination or work with a teacher or psychic. Pay attention to these special animals and how they figure in your life, as they may have important information for your spiritual journey. There are many different ways people can view their animal guides. They can be familiars, spirit animals, or even a patronus (to borrow a term from Harry Potter), but no matter what you call them, they are there to assist you in every way they can. Some people say they come from your ancestors or the supreme being or beings; whatever the case, treat them well and you will be greatly rewarded.

Water Animal Guides

Alligator and Crocodile: Much of the information about alligators and crocodiles as spirit animals is mixed together. Alligators are known to dig their own gator holes, which allow them to conserve necessary water even when the surrounding land is dry. They also build their own homes out of leaves and mud. This makes them both industrious and resourceful. As a guide, it is said they teach you to place importance on knowledge, initiation, healing, and protecting your own.

Both alligators and crocodiles have a spectacular mating display referred to as a "water dance." The males lower their bodies just beneath the surface of the water, then let out a strong low bellow from deep inside themselves. Their bodies shake and the water on the surface bubbles up like a beautiful fountain. This attracts any females in the area and discourages other males from challenging them.

In Hindu mythology, the god Varuna is said to ride on the back of a crocodile. Crocodiles are said to have amazing hearing and can even hear their children inside their shells before they are hatched. In ancient Egypt a crocodile god known as Sobek was responsible for protection, power, and fertility. He was also said to be responsible for weighing out the souls of the dead. If you feel connected to alligators and crocodiles, they may be trying to help you with courage, magic, strength, speed, resilience, or ancient power.

Beaver: This animal is most well-known for its building. Beavers are masters of strategy and engineering. They are constantly working to improve and maintain their homes and community projects. If beaver has appeared in your life, consider your contribution to your home, family, and community. Assess the progress you are making on your goals, and be sure to balance your time and attention accordingly. Despite its industriousness, the beaver is the largest of all rodents and some will view it as a pest. Those who have beaver as a frequent animal visitor may also have enemies, and they should be sure to pay attention to the intentions of those around them.

Crab: The crab is one of the most unusual animals around. The crab makes its home in its shell, so this animal can symbolically remind us how important our homes and family are. Unlike other animals, the crab moves sideways. Sideways movement emphasizes that sometimes the way forward isn't always straight ahead. Those with a connection to crab may find themselves having to find new and interesting ways around difficult situations in their lives. If one looks to tarot symbolism, one sees the crab again, this time on the tarot trump the Moon. The crab is also the symbol for the astrological sign of Cancer (June 21–July 22). Individuals with this sun sign often mimic some of the characteristics of the crab, namely cleverness, adaptability, and sensitivity.

Crane: This water bird symbolizes justice, creation, recovery, protection, and secrecy. The crane is especially revered in Asian culture and is frequently shown with pine trees and the sun. In the Celtic tradition, this bird aligns with death and the underworld.

Dolphin: Unlike most of the animals on this list, dolphins are mammals. The ancient Greeks saw the dolphin as a divine messenger. They have a complex system of sonar to guide them. People who have dolphin in their lives are harmonious inside and out. They are protective, intelligent, and playful.

Duck: Ducks have a special watery magic all their own. They are the most common waterfowl in most locales, and all breeds are known to swim. These birds are said to be linked with psychic energy, the astral realms, and the emotions. If they appear as a dream element or significant animal for you, consider the people, places, and things that are comfortable to you. This issue of comfort is at the core of duck magic. People even make pillows and mattresses from their feathers. Ducks were prized in ancient Egypt and China, as they are today. Pay special attention to the color and type of ducks you encounter, as it may help you to better understand their messages. The Norse goddess Sjofn was said to be accompanied by two ducks.

Dugong: Because of water pollution and coastal overdevelopment threatening their food supply and habitat, dugong are listed as an animal vulnerable to extinction. They are found in the coastal waters of Australia and East Africa. Often dugong and their cousin the manatee were mistaken for merfolk. As an animal guide, they are known to represent clear vision and a need for peace and calm. Dugongs are known to be gentle and friendly, and they can be called upon to help foster these qualities in yourself.

Frog: Frogs love the water; they are not to be confused with toads, who inhabit dry land. Frogs go from eggs to tiny swimming tadpoles to fully grown hopping adults. They show us the success and power that can unfold when a transformation occurs. Frogs are amphibians, which comes from the root words meaning "double life." They inhabit both land and water. This is the return of the concept of the liminal, or in-between, space where magic is known to happen. As a guide, they are known to represent magic, communication, fertility, and psychic ability. In ancient Egypt frogs were known to be sacred to Hadit, also known as Heqet, who helped Isis resurrect Osiris so that she could conceive Horus.

Gull: Because of their nature, some people view gulls as troublesome birds. Known as scavengers, gulls will take advantage of every opportunity to find food and resources. They are considered sacred to the Norse god Njord, who is said to rule over the sea and winds. Gulls are also said to be a beloved animal of the orisha Yemayá. Gulls are skilled communicators They use a complex system of calls and gestures to get their message across. The presence of these birds in your life may mean you need to pay attention to what you and others around you are saying. It can also be a sign that you need to speak up in certain situations in order to make your opinions known.

Heron: Heron as a totem can mean you would do well to develop self-reliance and good boundaries. While I was writing this book, I was thinking a lot about herons. I've seen quite a few in my lifetime, but just before I wrote these words, I managed to manifest one—taxidermy, of course—in the middle of downtown Brooklyn. It was waiting for an elevator just as I got off. The man who had brought it completely blocked the elevator door—did I mention this was about boundaries? Herons are wader birds. They thrive in shallow waters and marshlands. They are masters of this in-between space. They embody precision and also focus. Their bodies are adapted to these marshy locations. Herons have long skinny legs, long skinny necks, and sharp pointy beaks.

Hippopotamus: The hieroglyphics of Egypt use the hippopotamus to symbolize strength and vigor. In the mythological tale of Seth's fight with Horus, both of them are transformed into hippos. In addition, Egyptian mythology gives us the goddess Taweret, who has the body of a hippo, as well as parts of a crocodile and a lion. Taweret was seen as a mother goddess, a protector of women, in charge of fertility, childbirth, and motherhood. Hippopotami are seen as kind and gentle mothers themselves; even though they have difficulty swimming, they give birth in the water, in shallow protected places where their babies will be protected from the current. Taweret wasn't the only Egyptian deity associated with hippos—there were also Reret, Hedjet, and Ipet. In the African country of Nigeria, they are often depicted on masks and other ritual items in honor of Otobo, the water spirit, and some even see them as a symbol of the orisha Oshún.

Kingfisher: I recently had the joy of presenting at an event in Canada. The site was sublime, and behind me while I was giving my lecture was an amazing lake. When I had finished, many of the attendees came up and told me of the beautiful kingfisher that had appeared several times behind me. They are thought to be a symbol of great protection, prosperity, and peace. In Greek legend the Halcyone is a type of kingfisher that figures prominently. They are responsible for the phrase "halcyon days," which mean bright sunshiny days and calm waters. Kingfishers are also connected to the planet Jupiter, and if you feel this animal has a message for you, it could be one of good fortune.

Loon: Not a very graceful bird while on land, the loon is a master swimmer. This bird is constantly in the water. Its unique calls are its most easily identifiable feature. Some of their calls are like a wailing howl, others a laugh. Certain superstitions say that this call is a harbinger of death, while others believe it is simply a sign that rain is coming.

The loon is a master of breath work. It is also said to help you with dreams and altered states of consciousness. Both visions and messages are said to have great importance if you feel that the loon is taking a place in your spiritual life.

Manatee: There is a special place in my heart for manatees. Their slow and gentle way of being pleases and inspires me. Several years ago, I was going through a difficult time in my life and decided to take a trip to Florida to swim alongside the animals. Despite their large size, they were some of the most sweet and kind animals I have ever been around. On average, manatees can weigh upwards of 900 pounds, and when one of the largest ones began to swim towards me, I was unsure of how to act. As it got closer, it wrapped its arms around me and gave me what can only be described as a hug.

By nature these animals are warm and gentle, and they urge you to encourage these qualities in yourself. Long ago they were often mistaken for mermaids and mermen. They also move very slowly and gracefully, and thus are a reminder to take our time and remember our purpose. Manatees are a symbol of release and necessary change, as well as of learning how to trust those around us. People who have manatee as a sacred animal are often viewed as loners; the world can be too much for them, and sometimes they need to rest and recuperate.

Octopus: This animal is always on the move. It stays primarily on the very bottom of the ocean, making them one of the most grounded ocean animals. Octopuses are very skilled at changing colors and camouflaging themselves when necessary. If they are unsuccessful, they may ink the water around them in order to escape. If these are making themselves known to you, it could be an issue where you need to conceal yourself in order to avoid difficulties or make a diversion in order to get away from trouble.

Otter: Otters are definitely water creatures. They always make their homes near water and swim even faster than most fish. Otters love to play. If you have otter as a guide, you tend to make the best out of a situation and need to find time to enjoy yourself.

Pelican: Pelicans are distinguished by their scooping pouch and long bill. They use this for catching food, as opposed to storing it. These are some of the most buoyant birds. Both of these qualities help us to understand the benefits of resourcefulness and resilience. They tell us not to be discouraged by challenges or perceived disadvantages. Pelicans are also seen as selfless birds, and their presence may be urging you to spend time on self-care and personal enjoyment.

Penguin: Even though they are birds, penguins don't actually fly. They do move incredibly fast, however, swimming up to 25 miles an hour. Penguins are said to be helpers for astral travel and dreamwork. Because of their smart appearance, some suggest that penguins in your life could be a sign that you should dress elegantly or consider doing so. The birds have been known to jump up to six feet in the air up out of the water, landing squarely on their feet. These birds may appear in your life when you need to safely remove yourself from a situation. Alternately, they may be there to remind you that it is time to take a much-needed leap of faith. Like some of the animals on this list, penguins are known to mate for life, so if this animal keeps showing itself in connection to your relationship, it may be time to make a commitment and bring things to a deeper level. Emperor penguins are unique in that the male penguins care for the eggs after the female has laid them.

Seahorse: Seahorses are very graceful. Only the male seahorses birth the babies, making them unique in the animal kingdom. They can point to the importance of emotions and also responsibilities.

Sea Lion: Sea lions are brown, known to bark loudly, and walk on land with their flippers. The indigenous Northwest Coast people of North America often associate sea lions with abundance and wealth. Both the steller sea lion and the Australian sea lion are on the endangered species list. Please do what you can to help these beautiful creatures.

Seals: Seals lack visible ear flaps and wiggle on their bellies to move across land. Playful and imaginative, seals urge you to cultivate these qualities in your own life. Seals are more at home in the water. In Celtic and Scandinavian countries, seals feature prominently in folklore as shapeshifters, often called selkies. (See selkies in chapter 2's mythological water beasts section.)

There are many similarities between seals and sea lions. If these animals are appearing to you in dreams, visions, or the physical world, do your best to take note of exactly which sea lion or seal you are seeing. There are many different types, and each one carries its own unique message. To discover their special meaning for you, observe them when they appear.

Shark: Many of us, myself included, grew up with terrifying images of sharks in the popular media. Those that study sharks, however, paint a very different picture of an animal that is relatively peaceful. Shark magic is about safety, leadership, advancement, and confidence. They have an extraordinary sense of smell and may help you sniff out danger or opportunity when necessary. Shark teeth are worn as a symbol of strength and masculine energy; they are also said to help protect someone from drowning.

In indigenous Hawaiian culture, the shark is often regarded as an 'aumakua, or a deified ancestor spirit. Even today some still honor this connection, making a special effort to feed their 'aumakua when they go out to sea. A positive relationship with one's 'aumakua is said to both keep one safe from harm and help one find lots of fish to catch.

Starfish: Their very shape makes starfish quite magical. As a guide, they urge you to trust yourself, using both your traditional knowledge and intuition when presented with difficulties.

Stingray: Stingrays possess natural sensors that signal them when danger is near. If this animal is making itself known to you, it may be an indication to pay extra attention to your sixth sense and intuition.

Swan: The largest of all the waterfowl, the swan is both majestic and graceful. Swans can help us discover our own inner beauty. Just like in the classic tale "The Ugly Duckling," written in 1843 by Hans Christian Andersen, beauty is all about perception. If you are feeling drawn to swans as your animal totem, they will help you connect with psychic knowledge, prescience, and insight. In Hinduism the swan is considered an especially blessed bird and is described as the king of birds. Some say that swans are the animal of creatives, poets, visionaries, and innovators.

Turtles: Turtles are distinct from tortoises in that they always make their homes in and around water. There are numerous myths and legends surrounding the turtle. In Hindu cosmology the earth is said to sit on the back of four elephants standing on the shell of an enormous turtle. Many indigenous American groups had myths also stating that the earth sits on the back of a giant turtle, and North America is frequently referred to as Turtle Island. Turtles are known to live very long lives and can help us reconceive our relationship with time.

Walrus: Walrus medicine and magic is said to be nurturing and about protection, relaxation, and ease. More than any of the other animals in this chapter, walruses are truly about going with the flow. This animal moves slowly on land but is completely at home in the water. They swim using their entire body, yet are only able to dive in shallow water and stay under for a half hour at a time. Walruses hunt and travel with their herd and are fiercely protective of their young. They can both float and sleep in the ocean. Walruses were said to be sacred to the Norse god Hoenir, also called Ve.

Whale: The whale is an ancient creation symbol for many different cultures. There is a Haitian Vodou lwa called La Baliene who is sometimes seen as a whale; some envision her as an aspect of Erzulie. Whales are the largest mammals in the world. They help us understand our inner depths and power. Whale energy may mean that you feel things very deeply. Many Native people hold a special reverence for whales.

The narwal, also called a narwhale, is a whale that often has a large tooth protruding from its mouth that can grow up to ten feet long. Some people associate them with unicorns, and indeed these are the unicorns of the sea. These are animals of great magic and mystery. Said to be shapeshifters, they urge you to see the difference between appearance and reality in your life. Narwhals do not take well to being in captivity, so think about ways in your own life where you may feel defensive or caged.

The blue whale, the fin whale, and the beluga whale are all on the endangered species list. Please do what you can to help these majestic giants of the deep.

Animal Guide Meditation

Strengthening your connection to your animal guides can help you gain understanding and direction in every aspect of your life. Begin by finding a space to do your meditation, do your best to turn off all electronics and make sure you will be able to spend some time undisturbed. Gather all your items together and ready yourself by taking a deep breath and calming your mind.

ITEMS:

- blue cloth
- blue tealight candle
- glass candleholder
- water (this should correspond to the animal you are connecting with; for example, use sea water if your animal makes its home in the sea)
- photograph or other artistic representation of the animal
- water crystal or shell
- water incense (you can use an incense for the zodiac signs of Cancer, Pisces, or Scorpio, or one made from one of the water botanicals discussed in this book)

Take a little of the water and wipe down your table or sacred space. Place the blue cloth down and put the representation of your chosen animal in the center. Place the glass candleholder in front of it. Pour a small amount of water in the bottom of the candleholder, then add the candle. Light the candle and the incense. Hold the crystal or shell in your left hand. Focus your mind on your animal representation. If you feel yourself wanting to close your eyes, then do so. Pay close attention to what thoughts, images, or messages come to mind. Tell the animal that you would like to thank them for their help. Tell them that you will do what you can to help them. After your incense and candle have burned down, your meditation is complete. Gather the remnants of your working and dispose of them in an ecological manner. Record your thoughts and experiences in a notebook or Book of Shadows as soon as possible, while the information is fresh in your mind.

Animal guides can help to direct you on your magical path. They can do this by appearing literally in your life or in your dreams and journeywork. Pay careful attention to what they have to tell you. The connections you make don't have to be grandiose—even small things like finding a feather or hearing a howl can have meaning in your connections with animal guides.

PART
3

RECIPES, RITUALS
& SPELLCRAFT

Chapter 9

MAGICAL WATERS, BATHS, SALTS, AND WASHES

All water is magical, but some is more magical than others. This book has explored several different aspects of water as it occurs naturally, and now it will delve into water formulas and spells that you can bless and create for yourself. In my many years of magical practice, I have found that waters are some of the easiest spells you can create. After they have been formulated, you can use them in a variety of ways such as sprays, floor washes, and baths. You may wish to coordinate your working with the planetary correspondences for the days of the week.

Monday is ruled by and named after the moon. Doing magic on this day will help with psychic energy and ability, emotions, and goddess connections. The planet Mars is the ruler of Tuesday. This day is seen to resonate with power, courage, and strength. Wednesday corresponds to the planet Mercury. This is a good time for workings connected to communication, creativity, and change. Jupiter is connected to Thursday. Some Norse practitioners consider this Thor's day. It represents success in business, money, abundance, and healing. Friday is the day of Venus. It is for romance, love, fertility, and joy. Saturn is the ruler of Saturday, hence the name. It is said to be beneficial for magic dealing with protection, cleaning, clearing, and banishing. Sunday is ruled by our closest star, the sun. It is known to bring success, glory, and fame to your magic.

Day:	Ruled By:	Best For:
Monday	Moon	psychic energy, emotions, goddess connections
Tuesday	Mars	power, courage, strength
Wednesday	Mercury	communication, creativity, change
Thursday	Jupiter	business, money, abundance, healing
Friday	Venus	romance, love, fertility, joy
Saturday	Saturn	protection, cleaning, clearing, banishing
Sunday	Sun	success, glory, fame

Magical Waters

Eclipse Water: Eclipse magic is a strong and powerful thing. The energy of the sun and moon are condensed for a short period of time, and your magical working will benefit from this. While being able to view an eclipse is an exciting event, you do not need to see the event in order to harness its power. Eclipses are a great time to collect and harvest rainwater, dew water, storm water, or even snow if the situation presents itself. However, even if you don't have the opportunity to get water from the heavens at this time, you can still charge your own water with these energies representing a blending of the qualities of the sun and the moon. They represent a reversal of things, which can be useful for your own magical situations where things are stuck or going in a difficult direction. Creating this water is similar to the way you make either sun or moon water. Leave a jar of spring or tap water outside where the sun and moon's rays will touch it for at least 24 hours before and after the eclipse event. It will then be ready to use.

Florida Water: Contrary to what the name would lead you to believe, Florida water is not water from Florida. It is a cologne that has been in use for over 200 years to provide all-purpose blessings and success. Used by South American shamans, African healers, and even my Sicilian Great-Grandmother Providenza, it can be worn as a perfume (as the name implies) or in any multitude of other transformational ways. The original formula is unknown but seems to have undercurrents of lemon, lavender, and bergamot. It is a sweet citrus-based blend that is truly delightful. Many people have chosen to use it as they would a sage smudge or a quartz crystal for clearing out a space and amplifying whatever magic is happening. In my tradition of New Orleans Voodoo, the water is used as a gateway between the worlds. It is both centering and a way of connecting you with the invisibles. Typically it is applied to the hands, feet, and the back of the neck to make sure you are guided in the right direction with the right energy and mindset. Florida water can also be added to your ritual baths and floor washes.

The most well-known commercial preparation is made by the Murray & Lanman company. They have been making it the same way for over two centuries. Personally, this is the formula I like the best. However, many modern practitioners have chosen to make their own, and you can do so too with the following instructions. I prefer using essential oils for this recipe rather than fresh or dried herbs because that way you will save yourself the trouble of having to strain your mixture or run the risk of having chunky pieces in your final product. If possible, always use pure essential oils in your recipes; this will ensure that you end up producing a high-quality product. This particular recipe is best created on the eve of the full moon, which will allow you to capture the heightened energy of the time.

INGREDIENTS:

Glass bottle

1 cup vodka

3 tablespoons rose water

9 drops bergamot oil

9 drops orange flower oil

6 drops sage oil

6 drops lavender oil

6 drops rosemary oil

6 drops lemon oil

3 drops cinnamon oil

3 drops clove oil

Gather all the ingredients together. Begin by filling the bottle with the vodka. Next, add the rose water. Cap the bottle and shake well. Now add the bergamot, orange flower, sage, lavender, rosemary, lemon, cinnamon, and clove oils. Cap the bottle again and shake well. Next, if possible, take your bottle outside dig a hole in the earth and bury your bottle overnight. In the morning, go outside and dig up the mixture; now it is ready for use. Shake well before each use. The amount of alcohol in this recipe should keep it preserved, but please check it from time to time to make sure it has not gone off. If you are unable to bury your mixture in the ground, get a bucket and a bag of potting soil. Place the bottle in the bottom of the bucket and cover with dirt. Leave it outside or on a moonlit windowsill overnight, and then it will be ready for use.

Holy Water: In most instances people will want to obtain holy water from their local church. Often this can be obtained for free or for a nominal donation. I understand that many people have justifiable problems with the Catholic Church, so by all means, if you want to make your own holy water, go ahead. You might also consider using sacred water from another religion, such as Hindu water from the Ganges or something similar.

INGREDIENTS:

Spring water or water from a sacred site

Quartz crystal

Prayers and blessing words from your tradition

When making your own holy water, let your own practices be your guide. Maybe you want to go to a sacred well and charge that water with a prayer for the Goddess. Adding a quartz crystal will help amplify the energy of the water and attune it to higher vibrations. Your blessing will be guided by intuition and the things that you consider holy.

Moon Water: Simply put, moon water is water that has been blessed by the moon. You can use either the energies of the full moon or the new moon to charge up your water. Customarily the full moon is thought of as the most powerful time for manifestation magic, while the new moon is a good time to do spells and workings for growth and opportunity. You can magically charge your water by leaving a bottle, bowl, or chalice filled with water in a place where the moon's rays will be able to touch it—either outside or on a windowsill. For this process, you can use spring water, tap water, rainwater, or any other type of water you choose. The moon, like the element of water, is said to rule the emotions and psychic power. By charging your waters in this way, it will make them much more effective in your spells and workings.

Rose Water: Rose water is a sweet and refreshing element used in many different types of spells and potions. Magically it can be used in workings to generate love, romance, healing, psychic energy, and protection. It is also a beauty product that can be used as a moisturizer, toner, hair rinse, skin and face spray, and even as an ingredient in cooking. Rose water is readily available as a commercial preparation, and quite frankly this is the easiest way of obtaining it. However, you may wish to make your own recipe. Start with fresh organic petals that are not bruised. White petals are said to create an atmosphere of healing and calm, while red or pink flowers are said to stimulate passion and romance. Choose your blooms accordingly.

INGREDIENTS:

Large enamel or ceramic saucepan with a lid

Small bowl that will fit inside the saucepan

Small brick or flat rock

Spring water

1 quart or more of rose petals

15 ice cubes

Glass bottle or jar

Gather all your ingredients together. Place the brick or rock in the bottom of the pan and place the bowl on top of it. Surround the brick with the rose petals, making sure it is still sitting firmly. Pour the water into the pan until the rose petals are just barely covered. Next, place the inverted lid onto the pan, making a tight seal. Heat the pan until the water begins to simmer. Then place one ice cube at a time onto the lid. The inverted lid will contain the melted ice. When the first cube has melted, then add the next ice cube; repeat. Do not let all the water in the bottom of the pan evaporate. After about 10 minutes, you will have collected most of the usable rose water, so remove the pan gently from the heat and let it cool completely. If all goes well, your bowl should be full of rose water. Take this and pour it carefully into your glass bottle or jar. It is now ready to use in your magic.

Sun Water: This type of water receives a blessing from the sun, which has the power to impart joy, healing, and success. You can create this water by leaving a bottle, bowl, or chalice filled with spring water in a place where the sun's rays will be able to bless it. Leave it for at least 3 hours, and then it will be ready for use.

War Water: There are several different recipes for war water, or Mars water, as it is also called. It has long been a favorite of Hoodoo and folk magic practitioners for protection and removal of negativity and obstacles. Basically it is water with iron added. It was originally used to treat anemia and other disorders. War water can also be used in the process of launching your own psychic wars. This is considered a very powerful formula, and this type of work can be tricky ethically, so please proceed with caution. Psychic warfare and attack always have consequences; some even believe it comes back on you many times over. Making war water is a simple process but it does take some time. Tradition says to start this process on a Tuesday, which is sacred to Mars and the energy of war.

INGREDIENTS:

21 iron-cut nails (sometimes called masonry nails)

1 quart glass jar

½ cup storm water

½ cup tap water

Pinch of black salt

Small glass bottles (optional)

Place the iron nails into the jar. Mix the waters together. Fill the jar halfway with the storm and tap water. Next, add the black salt. Cover the jar and shake vigorously for 3 minutes. Place the lid on loosely so the air can escape. Place the jar in a dark corner, preferably somewhere cool where it will not be disturbed. After seven days, check it. If there is no mold or nastiness growing on it, add more water. If it looks funky, discard the mixture and start again. After adding more water, shake it up thoroughly, place the cap loosely back on top, and return it to the dark corner. Wait seven more days and check it again. If it looks like really rusty water with no mold or growth, it is now ready to use. Strain out the amount needed and save the rest for later. Once you have started this process, you can simply add more water to the jar when you start to run low. Some practitioners have war water jars that have been stewing for years. One traditional way of using this formula is to place it in a small glass bottle and throw it on the doorstep (so it breaks) or in the path of your enemy, then turn around and don't look back. Keep in mind there may be legal consequences if you use this method.

Willow Water: This water is used for healing and also for honoring the ancestors. Since ancient times, the bark from willow trees and various other plants rich in salicylates were utilized for pain relief and healing. In 1897 the Bayer Company began using salicylates in a chemical compound, which they then began to sell as aspirin.[43] Now the following formula is not to be ingested but can be used as a wash, bath, or spray on yourself or around your home to bring about relief from negativity, pain, and stress. It can also be used as an offering or to wipe down tombstones or mausoleums to honor the mighty dead.

---

43 Bethard, *Lotions, Potions, and Deadly Elixirs*, 129.

INGREDIENTS:

> 1 cup spring water
>
> 1 cup rainwater
>
> ¼ ounce white willow bark
>
> 3 drops lavender oil
>
> Strainer
>
> Saucepan
>
> Glass bottle or jar

Gather all ingredients together on your working altar or shrine. Place the saucepan on the stove and heat it over low heat. Next add the water; when it begins to simmer, then add the white willow bark. Cook for 15 minutes, then remove from heat and let the mixture cool completely. Strain into your glass bottle or jar, then add the lavender oil. Cover the bottle or jar and shake well. Now it is ready for use. Add the contents to a full tub of water. Use the mixture within seven to ten days, and by all means discard it sooner if it begins to become moldy or unpleasant.

Water Substitutes

I once wrote a post on my blog *Voodoo Universe* called "Fire: There Is No Substitute"—well, this is even more the case with the element of water. Humans can't live without it, and magically it carries its own special energy that compares to nothing else.

Overall, I think substitutes in any area of magic are a bit problematic. I know several of you reading this will probably want to seriously fight me. In my experience, part of the magical process is the hunt for rare and exotic ingredients, which may require traveling to new and exciting places. This is part of both the training and the journey. The quest is an integral part of the magic.

There are some substitutions that can be made for herbs or crystals relating to water. Lots of people recommend rosemary as a substitute for most herbs relating to protection and removal of negativity, while lavender is often used as a replacement for herbs relating to growth and success. Unfortunately, this may make things difficult for those seeking to obtain certain types of water to perform spells or workings. Luckily, through online sources almost every type of water is available.

Even if you can't find a readily available source, talk to people—maybe you have a relative or neighbor who might be traveling somewhere where they could get some ocean water or river water for you. Some of the best magical advice I have ever given is "make a friend." Otherwise, consider doing another type of spell or working where you are able to obtain the necessary ingredients.

While you may not be able to substitute anything for water but actual water, it does have a unique property of being able to make more water once you already have some in your possession. For example, if you have some rainwater or river water and you need a certain amount for a spell or working but you don't have enough, you can simply add some spring water or even tap water. The new creation will energetically still have the same properties as the original water, albeit slightly diluted. I find it interesting that a similar principle exists in science. Water is said to carry minute traces of everything it has come in contact with. Some have used this to argue that water actually has its own special kind of memory.

Sacred Baths

Using sacred baths is one of the most divine things a person can do. Immersing yourself in transformative waters allows you to change your destiny on every level. Sacred baths and bath salts can be crafted using a variety of different ingredients, and several formulas for doing so will be featured below. While many different traditions have time-honored formulas for crafting these baths, don't be afraid to make some of your own. It doesn't even necessarily require a bathtub: although it isn't ideal, a magical bath can also be taken in a washtub or even a large container.

Think of your ritual bath as your own personal cauldron that you are going to immerse yourself in. While you won't be cooking yourself in the traditional sense, you will be brewing up a whole new reality. Some people do have sensitivities, so please be sure to test how your skin reacts to the mixture before immersing yourself in the bath.

Simply start by asking yourself a few important questions. Foremost, why are you taking this bath? What is your focus? General guidelines are given for each of the baths here, but you will still want to personalize it for yourself. Maybe you want to add a favorite crystal or oil representing yourself or your astrological sign. This can help you better attune your own personal energy fields to the working. Having a clear focus is one of the most important things you can do in your spellwork. What other elements or components will you be adding to your bath? Do you want to set up a crystal grid in your bathroom or around your tub? Do you want to add incense or candles? Magic very often works on the principle of increase, and adding additional things to your ritual bath will most likely improve your chances for success.

Before you begin in earnest, be sure to prepare your bathroom and tub. They should both be physically and spiritually clean. In addition, your time in the bath should be free from outside distractions. You should also give some thought as to exactly when you are going to take your bath. While some of the formulas listed here are best prepared during the full or new moon, you will still need to decide precisely what time to get in the bath. There are planets that govern each hour of the day, and you may need to take these into consideration. You can find these out by consulting a professional astrologer or by searching online. By timing your bath or spell to correspond with the planet that is most likely to be helpful to your working, you will again improve your chances of success greatly. For example, a bath to bring love and romance into your life will be assisted if you take this during a time ruled by the planet Venus. The different days of the week also carry their own unique energy. Since this book focuses on water magic, I will start by saying that Monday is the day traditionally associated with water and the moon. Taking baths on this day will emphasize both your personal and spiritual connection to the element of water.

Astrology Baths

These baths are made with herbs and oils associated with the watery astrology signs Pisces, Scorpio, and Cancer. You can use them when you want to attract the qualities of these signs or to highlight the placement of these particular signs in your own astrology chart.

Pisces Bath: The astrological sign of Pisces (February 19–March 20) is said to be filled with creativity, imagination, kindness, compassion, psychic knowledge, insight, and romance. It is best to create this formula on the night before the full moon.

INGREDIENTS:

3 drops lavender oil

3 drops myrrh oil

¼ cup elderberry juice

2 cups tap water

1 cup spring water

1 cup ocean water

Large glass bottle or jar

Combine all ingredients in a large glass bottle or jar. Shake well to combine all the elements. Leave the jar outside or on a windowsill overnight where the full moon's rays will touch and bless it. In the morning the bath will be ready to use. If you are not going to use it immediately, place it in the refrigerator. For best results, use within 24 hours.

Scorpio Bath: The sign of Scorpio (October 23–November 21) is infamous for its mysterious complexity. It is a sign of great passion, energy, wisdom, and psychic ability. Often this sign is associated with transformation on a deep and powerful level.

INGREDIENTS:

3 drops patchouli oil

3 drops frankincense oil

6 drops rosemary oil

1 teaspoon vanilla extract

½ cup pomegranate juice

1 cup spring water

½ cup rainwater

Large glass bottle or jar

Add all the ingredients to the large glass bottle or jar. Shake vigorously until combined. Leave the jar outside or on a windowsill overnight where the full moon's rays will touch and bless it. In the morning the bath will be ready to use. Add the contents to a full tub of water. If you are not going to use it immediately, place it in the refrigerator. For best results, use within 24 hours.

Cancer Bath: The sign of Cancer (June 21–July 22) values the home and family above all else. It is a sign of great emotion, nurturing, caring, sensitivity, intelligence, and psychic power. One of Cancer-born individuals' superpowers is their insight and intuition. You can use this bath to highlight and focus on these gifts.

INGREDIENTS:

3 drops honeysuckle oil

6 drops jasmine oil

6 drops sandalwood oil

¼ cup lemon juice

1 cup spring water

1 cup river water

Large glass bottle or jar

Place the oils, juice, and waters into the large glass bottle or jar. Shake vigorously until combined. Leave the jar outside or on a windowsill overnight where the full moon's rays will touch and bless it. In the morning the bath will be ready to use. If you are not going to use it immediately, place it in the refrigerator. For best results, use within 24 hours.

Healing Baths

There is a long history of healing baths, and by using a few witchy ingredients it is easy to craft your own ritual baths for this purpose. Here are several different recipes. Feel free to use any or all of these formulas, testing first to make sure your skin isn't sensitive to the ingredients.

All-Around Ambrosia Bath: In several folk magic traditions and in African traditional religions it is a common practice to make a healing and protection bath with the herbs and plants that you find growing and thriving nearest your home. These can be either cultivated plants or even weeds. I remember once I was researching different traditional blessing baths from Cuba and came across an ingredient listed simply as ambrosia. This was before the days of the internet, so after much searching in deep academic libraries, I found a cross-reference that listed this herb with the common name of stinkweed. One man's stinkweed is obviously another man's ambrosia. The philosophy behind the inclusion of the herbs that grow near a person is that the earth, water, and other elements surrounding a person provide all the magic they will need to enhance their life. I recommend that everyone try this type of bath at least once to attune themselves to the sacred energy around them.

INGREDIENTS:

2 cups of fresh herbs, weeds, and plants gathered from close to your home

1 cup fresh basil

1 quart spring water

Large glass jar

Piece of cheesecloth

10 drops sandalwood oil

10 drops copal oil

1 cup Florida water (either a commercial formula or one made from the recipe listed in this book)

1 piece clear quartz crystal

Place the herbs into the jar. Cover completely with the spring water. Loosely put the lid on the jar. Leave the jar outside or on the windowsill where the sun's rays will touch and bless it for the next 24–36 hours. Bring the jar back inside and place it on your working altar. Strain all the herbs and plants out of the water using the cheesecloth. You can then dispose of the herbs—the best place to do this is in the woods underneath a large tree. Take the remaining liquid and add the sandalwood and copal oils, the Florida water, and the clear quartz. The bath is now ready to use. After seven days any unused portion should be discarded.

Bitter Healing Bath: In some African traditional religions, certain herbs are considered sweet and others bitter. The bitter ones are said to heal from illness, remove all bad vibes, and clear out all blockages. This formula includes several of these plants along with others designed to promote health. Use this bath during the new moon to help with healing.

INGREDIENTS:

¼ cup basil leaves

¼ cup sage leaves

¼ cup parsley leaves

Natural cloth bag

1 cup spring water

1 cup tap water

1 cup holy water

Large bowl

6 drops eucalyptus oil

First gather all ingredients on your working altar or shrine to bless them. Place the basil, sage, and parsley leaves in the cloth bag. Heat waters in a saucepan until they begin to simmer. Remove from heat. Put the cloth bag into the bowl and carefully pour the water over it. By doing this you are making an infusion. Add the eucalyptus oil. The mixture should be covered with a clean natural fiber cloth and left overnight. In the morning remove the herb bag and discard it. The bath is now ready to use. For best results, use the mixture within 24 hours.

Emotional Healing Bath: Maybe you are healing from a loss or a dysfunctional past; whatever the case, this bath will help you heal from difficult emotional situations. Water is the element of the emotions and transformation, and this bath speaks directly to that. It is best created during the full moon, but use it as often as necessary when you are feeling down, and remember to always seek professional help and support for depression, and keep in mind you are not alone.

INGREDIENTS:

Large glass jar

1 cup spring water

1 lemon, sliced thin

Handful of fresh violet blossoms

3 drops hyssop oil

6 drops lavender oil

6 drops bergamot oil

3 drops rosemary oil

Cheesecloth for straining

1 cup Florida water (either a commercial formula or one made from the recipe listed in this book)

Gather all ingredients together on your working altar or shrine. Add the spring water to the jar. Next add the slices of lemon and violet blossoms. Now add the hyssop, lavender, bergamot, and rosemary oils. Cover the jar loosely, then leave it outside or on a sunny windowsill for 24 hours so the sun's rays will have a chance to heat and bless the mixture. Next, open the jar and strain the mixture through the cheesecloth. Add the Florida water. The mixture is now ready for use. Use within the next 21 days for best results.

Bath Salts

Bath salts are a more long-term magical craft. Unlike the water baths, you can make them well in advance of when they will be needed. Because the base is primarily made of sea salt, these baths are best used for spiritual cleansings and removing negativity. I like to use essential oils in conjunction with the salt rather than the herbs because this way you save yourself the trouble of cleanup or straining the mixture so as not to clog your drains.

Save Me Sea Salt Mixture: This mixture contains oils and salt designed to honor the goddesses of the seas.

INGREDIENTS:

    1 cup sea salt

    Large glass jar

    7 drops sandalwood oil

    7 drops spearmint oil

    7 drops galangal oil

    7 drops myrrh oil

Place all the necessary ingredients on your working altar or shrine. Pour the salt into the jar. Next add the sandalwood, spearmint, galangal, and myrrh oils. Place the lid on the jar and shake vigorously. Leave the jar overnight where the moon's rays will touch and bless it. Now it is ready to use. Place 3 or more tablespoons into your bathwater. Climb in, then relax and focus on the Goddess as you soak.

Lots of Love Bath Salts: This traditional formula to attract love and romance is best created on the eve of the full moon. The focus should be on attracting the best possible love to you. It should be general and not directed at any particular individual.

INGREDIENTS:

    1 cup Himalayan pink sea salt

    Large glass jar

    6 drops rose oil

    6 drops orange blossom oil

    6 drops amber oil

    1 small piece moonstone

Gather all ingredients together on your working altar or shrine. Place the sea salt into the jar. Next add the rose, orange blossom, and amber oils one at a time. Lastly add the moonstone. Shake well and leave the jar overnight outside or on a windowsill where the moon's rays will touch and bless it. Now it is ready to use. Place 2 tablespoons of the mixture into a full bath (leave the moonstone in the jar). When you are done with the entire mixture, take the moonstone and throw it into a moving body of water such as a river or stream.

Whole Healing Bath Salts: Please be sure to seek traditional medical help when you are in need of healing; magic alone is never a substitute for this. With that said, the following bath salts contain healing oils and salt to help place you on the path to good health.

INGREDIENTS:

    1 cup sea salt

    Large glass jar

    6 drops eucalyptus oil

    6 drops rosemary oil

    6 drops lavender oil

    6 drops sandalwood oil

    3 drops cypress oil

Get all the ingredients together on your working altar or shrine. Pour the sea salt into the jar. Then add the eucalyptus, rosemary, lavender, sandalwood, and cypress oils to the jar one at a time, shaking the mixture after each addition. Place the lid on the jar and leave overnight outside or on a windowsill where the moon's rays will touch and bless it. Now it is ready to use. Add 3 tablespoons of the mixture to a full bath as warm as you can tolerate. Get in and soak. Focus on all the ills that have been bothering you soaking out through your skin and eventually down the drain. Repeat this bath as often as necessary.

Sacred Floor Washes

Herbal floor washes are a mainstay in African traditional religions. In many ways they are like a ritual bath that goes all over your entire home. By utilizing these washes, you will be able to create a positive atmosphere in your space for all who enter. It is best to use a special dedicated bucket for these floor washes. What I recommend, unless otherwise specified, is to do a normal type of cleaning on your space with products like ammonia, pine, or other traditional cleaning products, and then follow up with your formulas for spiritual cleansing. If you don't have time to wash the floors the good old-fashioned way on your hands and knees, you may wish to alternatively put these washes into a spray bottle and use them that way.

Protection Floor Washes

Some of the most important work you can do as a spiritual person is for protection.

Block Buster Floor Wash: This is a very common formula in Hoodoo and many variants of African traditional religion. It is designed to quickly remove all blockages and difficulties that stand in your way. Often it is followed by a wash used to open the path to success.

INGREDIENTS:

1 gallon spring water

Large glass or enamel bowl

1 small piece High John the Conqueror root

6 drops rosemary oil

6 drops peppermint oil

6 drops lemon oil

6 drops frankincense oil

Add the water to the bowl, then add High John the Conqueror root and the oils. Leave the bowl outside or on the windowsill where the rays of the new moon will bless it. In the morning when you bring it inside, it is ready to wash down your home and ritual space. If you have some left over, you may choose to save it in a bottle and use up until the next new moon. When you have used all of the mixture, take the High John root out and leave it at the crossroads or anyplace where two or more roads meet, then turn and leave without looking back.

Double Reversible Floor Wash: If you feel that there is a lot of negativity around you, one logical solution is to send that energy back from where it came. Double-action reversible candles, oils, and floor washes are very popular in the tradition of La Regla Lucumi, more commonly known as Santeria.

INGREDIENTS:

3 cups spring water

1 cup tap water

1 cup Florida water

Bucket

9 drops rosemary oil

9 drops rue oil

9 drops sandalwood oil

Small handful of sea salt

Gather all ingredients together in your ritual space. Pour the waters into the bucket. Next, add the rosemary, rue, and sandalwood oils, then add the sea salt. Stir counterclockwise until the mixture is well combined. Now you may use it to wash down your floors, windows, corners, and walls. If you have been having trouble sleeping, try washing underneath your bed. When you are done, dispose of any unused mixture by flushing it down your toilet.

Blue Velvet Floor Wash: This formula is designed to leave an aura of peace and protection throughout your environment. It is like a powerful psychic blanket that you can lay over your space.

INGREDIENTS:

1 gallon spring water

1 gallon tap water

5-gallon bucket

¼ cup lemon juice

¼ cup laundry bluing (or 9 small laundry bluing balls)

Arrange all ingredients together on or in front of your working altar. Pour the waters into the bucket, then add the juice and the laundry bluing. Stir to combine. Use the mixture to wash down your floors, paying special attention to the corners and thresholds. Dispose of any leftover water when done.

Healing Floor Washes

Healing floor washes can be used to prevent disease or help heal diseases that may be present. Use them as often as necessary to keep yourself and your home healthy.

All-Heal Floor Wash: This is a great all-purpose healing formula that you can utilize for either prevention or cure.

INGREDIENTS:

Large earthenware pot

1 quart spring water

1 cup freshly grated coconut

1 cup rosemary leaves

1 cup eucalyptus leaves

9 drops sandalwood oil

Cheesecloth or muslin fabric for straining

Place the pot on the stove. Heat water over medium heat until it begins to simmer. Add the coconut, rosemary, eucalyptus, and sandalwood. Reduce heat to low and simmer for 20 minutes, then remove from heat. When the mixture has cooled, strain it and discard the herbs and coconut. Take the remaining liquid and add it to your regular wash water for the floor. Use the mixture to thoroughly wash down doorways, floors, and windows. Dispose of any remaining wash water outside when you are done.

Healing Waters Floor Wash: This recipe includes many different kinds of waters to help craft a healing space. It may take a little bit of effort to find all of the necessary ingredients, but it will be well worth your time. Feel free to use this on your floors as well as your doors and windows both inside and outside of your home. It also makes a good wash for cleansing your ritual tools and crystals.

INGREDIENTS:

    1 cup holy water

    1 cup spring water

    1 cup tap water

    1 cup rose water

    1 cup ocean water

    6 drops sandalwood oil

    6 drops myrrh oil

    6 drops jasmine oil

    Peel of 1 lemon

    Large glass jar

Combine all ingredients in the large glass jar. Shake well. Leave the jar outside or on the windowsill for 24 hours, where both the sun and moon's rays can bless and charge it. You can then use the mixture to clean the spaces in your home. Use within seven days. Repeat as necessary.

Crafting your own magical waters, washes, and baths requires some personal work and some action. Once you figure out which ones you would like to focus on, you will be able to see how these watery treasures can bring about positive change in all areas of your life. For best results, you should use the waters, baths, and washes on both yourself and your surroundings, such as your home, yard, office, etc.

Chapter 10

WATER IN DIVINATION
AND DREAMS

Divination and dreams are inherently watery. They are deep, elusive, and mysterious. By calling on the elemental power of water, we can gain true insight and understanding. In dreams water can manifest in as many ways as it does in waking life. There can be rivers to cross, waterfalls to dance in, and oceans to sail. Each one tells us something different about the situations that are occurring in our lives. Water can also be used to help understand the messages that come through divination. There is water-based scrying such as well gazing, tools like tarot that feature watery imagery, and dowsing rods and pendulums that can be used to tell the future or find actual water.

Throughout almost eight thousand years of history, the dowsing rod has been used to find things, most specifically water. The process, called rhabdomancy, is unclear in its origins. However, it has been successfully used by empires, governments, and the military to find necessary water. The rods have been said to be symbolic of the Egyptian pharaoh's scepter or even Poseidon's trident, while phallic implications of power and sexuality are evident as well. Dowsing rods are said to have been used by the Queen of Sheba, King Solomon, Queen Cleopatra, and Marco Polo. In the nineteenth century, many people practiced dowsing for a variety of purposes. The common belief today, however, has classified dowsing as a psychic process that is not grounded in traditional science. Somewhere along the way dowsing became attached to magic. During the Spanish Inquisition dowsing was considered "water witching" and was punishable by death. The Catholic Church repeatedly denounced dowsing, and Martin Luther declared it a mortal sin. Despite this, the methods still live on today.

Water Symbolism in Dreams and Journey Work

Sometimes water has a message to tell us. One of the ways it does this is by appearing in our dreams or journey workings to help us find our way. Obviously, everyone's dreams have their own personal significance, but there are some general guidelines for interpreting symbolism that one can follow.

Sigmund Freud in his *Interpretation of Dreams* (1913) wrote quite a bit about water both generally and specifically. Over a hundred years later, some of this seems a little basic. Yes, of course, if your blanket falls off in the middle of the night, you may feel like you are slipping into the water; if you are thirsty in real life, you may dream that this thirst is quenched; or water in a dream may simply represent that you need to go to the bathroom. Freud also asserts that dreams of floating or swimming through narrow passages may represent being in the womb or the birth process.[44] Alter-

---

44   Freud, *Interpretation of Dreams*, 100–244.

natively, there are the conclusions of Carl Jung, whom I personally prefer to Freud, in his analysis of dream symbols and archetypal representations. For more than half his life, Jung lived on the water. Water, he believed, was the symbol of "the collective unconscious." Jung aligned water in dreams with feminine energy.[45]

Pay special attention to how you are interacting and feeling about the water present in your dreams; this can unlock its unique message. Water is about potential, and how you react to this potential may give you insight.

Lakes: According to Zen Buddhism, lakes can symbolize meditation and the mind. In general, dreaming of lakes represents your life, specifically your emotional state. If the lake is calm, you are experiencing inner peace; if it is turbulent, there may be some issues or emotional disorder.

Ocean: In many ways, seeing or being near the ocean in your dreams can symbolize the unknown. Pay attention to the feeling you associate with this locale while you are dreaming; if it is tumultuous and you are feeling anxiety or fear, maybe there is something hidden that you are nervous about discovering.

Rain: Rain in your dream could be indicative of sadness or grieving. However, rain also is indicative of fertility, and it could mean new abundance and success coming into your life. A question to ask yourself is about the intensity of the rain in the dream. Are you caught in an extreme storm or is the rain just a subtle backdrop?

45   Jung, *Dreams*, 145.

Rivers: Rivers can either be rough or calm. Depending on which one you are dealing with in your dreamspace, the messages can vary. In many ways, rivers are transportation routes, and seeing one in your dream could mean there is an upcoming move or some sort of travel down the road for you. If in the dream you remember crossing a river, this could mean that you are facing a challenge or a transition in your life that you will be able to navigate successfully. A river of clear water may be symbolic of happiness and satisfaction in your life, while a dry riverbed can mean that you are feeling unsatisfied or being deceived in some way. Freud equated rivers with the father figure in a person's life. Jung believed that rivers in dreams could also represent the neverending journey of self-discovery and being at one with your destiny.

Springs: Springs can symbolize newness and opportunity in your dreams. Alternatively, there could be an issue with your bladder. Dreams can be quite literal sometimes.

Storms: Dreaming of storms can mean that you are having difficulties expressing your emotions. They can also mean obstacles or delays in your path.

Swamps: The swamp is a place of in-between. Most often swamps are characterized by stagnant water. Dreaming of yourself in the swamp could mean that you are stuck in your current situation. Stagnant water can also signify insincerity in your feelings and actions.

Waterfalls: Waterfalls in dreams are said to represent great joy, abundance, and vitality. They can also be symbolic of the need to rest and recharge, perhaps even take a vacation.

Dowsing Rods

Dowsing rods aren't just for finding water; they are also very useful for divination. They allow you to become aware of different energies and currents in the atmosphere. Functioning as a conduit for psychic energy, they work very well for some people. You can use one rod or two for divination. Traditionally they were made out of sticks of hazel or willow trees, while today it is common to use copper. It is interesting to note that both copper and willow have been associated specifically with the element of water. These materials will allow the psychic energy to flow most excellently.

My best advice for using the rods is to begin by setting up your ritual altar or working area. Be sure to include ritual items to represent each of the elements. Hold the rods gently in your hands. Sometimes it helps if you shake your hands vigorously before you begin. Next, do your best to clear your mind of extraneous thoughts. This can be helped by burning sandalwood or other incense used for focus and meditation. Then proceed by speaking aloud your intentions. You can ask the rods to show you what a yes response from them will look like. The rods may come together, move apart, spin around quickly, or stay still. Pay close attention to the clues the dowsing rods give you.

Next, ask the dowsing rods to show you what a no answer will look like. Again, pay close attention to their movements. When you have observed these two hopefully different states, you are now ready to begin. Ask the rods if they are able to give you answers to your questions at this time. If the answer is no, put the rods away and try again later. If yes, you can ask your first question aloud. This should be a simple question that can be answered easily with a yes or no response.

Pendulums

Dowsing can also be done with a pendulum. If you are just beginning, try both methods out and see which works best for you.
Both pendulums and rods can be made with a variety of materials.
It may be that you prefer a particular material or method over the
others. It could also be that certain methods are more successful
for you. When starting out I recommend using them on a regular
basis to ask simple questions like "Will I get rained on today?" to
test out your success rate with dowsing. This will help you have a
better idea of what is going on when you use this method for more
serious questions.

Wax and Water Scrying

Water can conform to the shape of whatever vessel you put it into.
This makes it uniquely suited for divination and scrying. Scrying
is a form of divination; also called "peeping," it allows the mind to
see messages and information through shapes and symbols. Water
scrying is a form of hydromancy, or divination with water. You can
also divine with water by throwing offerings in it. Traditionally it
was thought that if your offering sank to the bottom of the water,
your wishes would be granted.

The fact that water can reveal things to us may be seen throughout both history and folklore. Even ancient sites like Bath were
used as a place to communicate with the dead and the otherworld.
In ancient Greece there was a shrine to Demeter where visitors
would lower a mirror down into the springs to determine the
health of a sick person. The mirror was said to show the person
either alive or dead. Aristotle wrote about a fountain in Sicily

where visitors threw notes into the water. If the notes floated on top of the water, they were said to come true.

In many ways water can function as a mirror both literally and figuratively. For better or worse, water provides a reflection—albeit a distorted one. It allows us to see things and feel things one would not otherwise have access to. The magic of transformation may be seen in these reflections. A mirror is a portal, just like the water. One can find their way to mysterious places where things are not always exactly as they seem.

The easiest way to water scry is to obtain a dark-colored bowl or container and fill it with water. Most often people use spring water, but feel free to use tap water, ocean water, river water, or whatever you feel drawn to using. It may help to charge your water overnight with the energy of the moon. You can even purchase special black water for this process, which gets its dark color from fulvic acid produced by the biodegration of dead organic matter. It contains extra minerals and electrolytes. The bottom line is that you can use many different things for scrying. I know some people who use plain water with the addition of ink, and even one hair-dresser friend who will tell the future from your shampoo bubbles.

Then, when you are ready, do your best to clear your mind, enter a meditative state, and gaze at the water. Some prefer to focus on the bottom of the bowl, while others say messages come from just below the surface. Try both and see what method works the best for you. The symbols you see can be interpreted using the same methods as tea leaf reading or dream interpretation, but ultimately you are in charge of what those images mean to you.

If you are having difficulty, it may help to dim the lights or perform some journey work beforehand. Do not try to rush the process; most worthwhile endeavors take time and effort. In any case, be sure to take note of what you see, as the meanings may not be immediately clear but instead may choose to unfold in the coming days or weeks. Water can be used as a scrying or divination tool all on its own or with the addition of wax or even metal.

Amethyst Scrying Bowl

Amethyst is one of the stones that is most often used for psychic power and connection. This makes it a natural choice for use in your water scrying bowl.

INGREDIENTS:

Black natural fabric cloth (preferably silk or cotton)

1 small black or dark blue ceramic or glass bowl

4 small white candles with candleholders

4 drops sandalwood oil

1 small mirror

1 small amethyst crystal

1 cup spring or well water

Matches or a lighter

Prepare a special place to do your scrying and begin by making sure your area is clean before you lay the cloth out. Place the bowl directly in the center of your cloth. Place the candles in their holders in each of the four directions, representing earth, air, fire, and water. On each candle place a drop of the sandalwood oil. In the bottom of the bowl place the mirror, and then put the amethyst on top of the mirror. Close the curtains or shades and turn out the lights. Darkness will help the process; some people even choose to wear a veil to help with prophetic messages. Light the candles.

Slowly pour the water into the bowl. Now do your best to clear your mind. You may wish to say a prayer, a blessing, or a statement of your intent. Then gaze into the water.

Wax Scrying

People also perform divination in water using wax to gain answers and insight. It is another type of scrying where you will get information from what you see in the wax. If you would like to try this yourself, here are some basic instructions.

INGREDIENTS:

> Dark-colored shallow scrying bowl (glass or ceramic)
>
> 1 cup water (moon, well, and river water work well)
>
> 1 white taper candle
>
> Matches
>
> Paper
>
> Fireproof bowl, ashtray, or dish

Dim the lights and draw the curtains in your room. Gather all items together on your altar or shrine. Place the bowl in the center of your space. Write down all your questions on the paper. Light the candle and very carefully drip the wax into the water as you state your question or focus on it silently (try not to burn yourself or anything else with the flame and wax). Let the candle drip into the water until it begins to form a shape or shapes. Then snuff the candle out and rest it in the fireproof dish. Next, take as much time as you need to meditate and study the shapes that have formed, recording your impressions on the paper. If you would like to ask additional questions, remove the wax shapes that have materialized in the water and begin the process over again. Make sure you have taken notes on all the questions and the responses you have received, then dispose of all the leftover wax in the trash and pour the remaining water out underneath a large tree. If you need more information on the shapes you are finding, consider consulting a book about dream symbolism or tea leaf reading; the interpretation of the signs and shapes you find there will be helpful in your process.

Tea Leaf Reading

Tasseomancy, more commonly known as tea leaf reading, is another way of using water in connection with divination. It is an ancient art that grew out of scrying practices that began in the Middle Ages. Similar to scrying, the future is told by reading the shapes and symbols that are left in the cup after drinking some tea. The practice can also be done with coffee, but it is less popular. For best results, you must start with a teapot and some loose tea. The tea must be stirred, steeped, and then poured out into the cups. The questioner can ask to find out information about a specific issue or to just generally know what the future looks like via the leaves. While drinking, the seeker can focus on the nature of water.

In *Tea & Tasseomancy* by K. Henriott-Jauw, she talks about drinking in waves, writing, "It was flowing into my mouth like the currents of the sea. I thought of the ocean and her connection to all shores."[46] When you are done drinking the tea, turn the cup upside down onto the saucer. Then turn the cup three times in a clockwise motion. Lift up the cup—now you are ready to scry what you see there. Any shapes, figures, or symbols you see will be relevant to your question. You must do your best to open your

---

46 Henriott-Jauw, *Tea & Tasseomancy*, 16.

mind and allow the messages to make themselves known. Like any good divination system, if you are ready to begin working with this, you must practice. Experiment with different tea blends and cups to see which ones provide the most effective results.

Holey Stones

Holey stones are rocks that have been worn down by the water, slowly creating a hole. While tradition says you are supposed to randomly find the stone in order for the magic to work, there are several places to look that will improve your odds. The rocks occur naturally in southern England, Denmark, Germany, the Netherlands, Canada, the USA, and even in Egypt.

Also referred to as hag stones, witch stones, Odin stones, adder stones, fairy stones, and other names, they are said to carry special powers. Long used in folk magic and Hoodoo, they are employed in a whole host of situations.

Holey stones are commonly used in magic and workings about ancestors and the dead. They can be used to keep away unwanted energies from beyond. You can do this by placing a hag stone in your pocket, hanging one by your bed, or tucking one beneath your threshold. If you are going to be using them for an extended period of time, make sure to rinse them in spring water periodically (during the full moon if at all possible) to make sure they retain their maximum effectiveness. You can also leave them as offerings on your ancestor altar to make sure only the most helpful dead come and take advantage of the space.

These stones have their own folklore throughout the world. Some traditions see them as viewfinders into the other realms.

They can be used for scrying either on their own or when placed into a bowl of water.

These stones can be worn directly on your person or hung in the doorways and windows to help ward off negativity and the evil eye. In some places these were even known as hex stones that would work to catch or trap any hex sent your way. Consequently, this kind of protection magic wasn't just used for people, but for animals such as livestock, buildings, and even boats facing danger on the sea.

One of the most famous holey stones is the Tolmen Stone. Located in Dartmoor National Park in England, the stone is the stuff of many legends. The very word breaks down in the Celtic language to *tol*, which means "hole," and *maen*, "stone." It lies near the edge of the North Teign River. Early Druids are said to have used the stone for purifications and water blessings. The stone features an opening of approximately 40 inches, and anyone who passes through it is said to be cured of rheumatic disorders like arthritis and gout. Coincidentally or not, this area of the United Kingdom is one of my favorite places in the world. I was fortunate enough to experience its magic as a young child and have been enchanted ever since. If you have the opportunity to visit here, I highly recommend it.

In Scotland on Orkney Island there are also some famous holey stones known as the Orkney Standing Stones. It is in one of these large holey stones that lovers are said to reach their hands through and pledge devotion, love, and fidelity in traditional handfasting or marriage ceremonies. If they break these promises, they are said to face retribution from this world and the next.

It isn't just Celtic folklore that features these holey treasures; they are also said to hold a special significance in Italian magic. In this area these are also seen as gateways to the Faery realms and are said to attract fairies and get them to do your bidding. In Italy these sacred stones are said to be a favorite of the goddess Diana.

The fact that these marvels are also called adder stones points to another part of the mythology surrounding them. Some people believe that the holes in these stones were not caused by water but instead by snakes. There are legends that say this was created by the bite of a snake, while others claim it was done by a group of snakes banding together. The latter theory is furthered by the Welsh Gaelic name for these rocks, Glain Neidr, which simultaneously means serpent's stone, serpent's glass, and Druid's egg. On the high holiday of Beltane, snakes were said to gather and form a ball with a hole in the center. Even Pliny, the ancient historian, mentioned these serpent eggs in his *Natural History*, saying:

> The Druids tell us, that the serpents eject these eggs into the air by their hissing...and that a person must be ready to catch them in a cloak, so as not to let them touch the ground; they say also that he must instantly take to flight on horseback, as the serpents will be sure to pursue him, until some intervening river has placed a barrier between them. The test of its genuineness, they say, is its floating against the curent of a stream, even though it be set in gold. But, as it is the way with magicians to be dexterious and cunning in casting a veil about their frauds, they pretend that these eggs can only be taken on a certain day of the moon; as though, forsooth, it depended entirely upon the human will to make the moon and the serpents accord as to the moment of this operation.[47]

47   Pliny (the Elder), *The Natural History of Pliny*, 389.

Whichever way you choose to use holey stones, it is clear that they are deeply and literally influenced by the water that creates them. It is as if the water has created a portal where magic can happen.

Hanging Holey Stone Charm: In almost all the areas they are found, holey stones are used to make protective charms and amulets. The most common one involves the use of a key. If you would like to create one for yourself, the instructions follow. Traditionally this was done with nine holey stones, but you can use fewer if necessary. As I mentioned, the stones that are randomly found hold the most power. Do your best to find as many as you can. A charm similar to this one dating from the 1800s is housed in the Natural History Museum in London, England.

ITEMS:

1 antique key

1 or more holey stones

1 cup spring water

1 cup ocean water

1 yard of red cord or ribbon

This working is best done outside or over your sink. Begin by holding the key and the stone in your left hand. Pour the waters over the key and the stone. Next, make a loop in the top of the ribbon and tie it. Then wrap the other end of the ribbon around the stone, going through the hole at least three times. Then knot the ribbon. Repeat with the other holey stones if you have them, then tie the key to the ribbon and cut off any excess ribbon. Now the charm is ready to hang up near your doorway or window to help protect and purify your home.

Crystal Grids with Water

Crystal grids have become very popular of late. You can use the grid to charge up your sacred waters and blends. You may also choose to create a crystal grid with water-influenced crystals.

Water Crystal Grid

If you like, you can make a basic crystal grid to spiritually charge your tarot cards, runes, dowsing rods, or other divination tools.

ITEMS:

Quartz crystal gem elixir

Blue or white natural fabric cloth

Glass candleholder

Small blue candle

Matches or a lighter

Divination tools (tarot cards, runes, dowsing rods, or similar)

2 blue kyanite points

2 pieces azurite

Lightly wipe down the space where you will be doing the working with some of the gem elixir. Cover the space with your cloth. Place the candleholder in the center of your cloth. Pour a few drops of the gem elixir in the bottom of the holder, then place the candle on top. Light it. Put your cards, runes, or other divination tool in the place between you and the candle. At the top of the cloth, in line with the candle and your tools, place one of the kyanite points. Directly opposite it, in front of you on the cloth, place the other kyanite point facing the other one. In the far left and right corners of the cloth, forming a 4-point cross, you will place the two pieces of azurite. While the candle burns, sit in front of the space and focus your energy on your divination tools. If you like, you may recite a power chant or mantra. Stay until the candle has burned out. When this is done, your divination tools will be recharged and ready to use again. You may repeat this grid whenever you feel the need.

Tarot

While I don't recommend actually getting your deck wet, you can use a tarot deck in many ways when doing different kinds of water divination magic. As I outlined in chapter 5, the suit of cups, along with other individual cards such as the Moon, is significant for this type of elemental work and is associated to water. Here are a few examples:

Tarot cards that represent your genuine desires can be used as part of your altar or shrine for the water element. You can use a reproduction, one of your actual cards, or an old card. When I have a deck that has been well used, I often retire it and break up the cards to utilize in this way.

You can place a significant cups card under your pillow at night to receive insight in your dreams. This could be a card that has been coming up repeatedly in your readings or one that represents the situations that you wish to receive in your life. Be sure to have a notepad and pen ready when you wake up so you can make note of what you learned. This is a great exercise to do on a regular basis, especially if you are just beginning to work with tarot.

Oils and herbs representing the tarot card you are focusing on can be made into an incense blend or oil. You can then wear this to attune with the energy throughout your day. There are several recipes for oils that evoke water's energy throughout this book. I was recently sorting through my magical drawers and found an old package of Ten of Cups incense. This can be burned to bring about great joy, happiness, and success in the home, representing all of the benefits this card stands for. This could also be done for the Ace of Cups, the Two of Cups, or any of the other cups cards you are trying to connect to. If you can't find these blends ready-made, consider substituting rose or jasmine incense.

Water can play a powerful part in divination and dreams. It can give us a better understanding of ourselves and the complex situations being navigated throughout existence. When water is present in dreams, it is almost as if a subtle puzzle is being presented to our unconscious selves. When decoded, these messages can give great insight to what is going on in our waking lives. The same can hold true for divination with water and things like tarot or dowsing rods.

Chapter 11

WATER SPELLS
AND OTHER MAGIC

Actual water in its most common form is used in almost all types
of magic. However, water as an element also corresponds to specific types of magic like love, healing, memory, ancestors, and
more. Many of the cross-cultural deities we have looked at in this
book also have influence over these domains. I have spoken about
the orisha Oshún and the goddess Aphrodite who both possess
great love magic, and the ancestors who, in addition to taking
water on their altars and shrines, are in African traditional religions often seen to travel through water to deliver messages.

In this chapter I will share with you some of my favorite spells
and workings focusing on these areas and more. Actual water may
or may not be included in each one. Please try to be mindful that
magic is about opening up yourself to the best of all possibilities
and aligning yourself with your true destiny. Make sure that you
are making yourself available to these situations rather than tying
yourself to one specific outcome.

CHAPTER 11

Love Spells

Love can be an elusive delight. It used to be when I would sit down to give someone a psychic reading, I would ask, "Is this about love?" In my experience, this is the topic that people want to know about more than any other area of their lives. Many people turn to magic because of issues with love. In many ways, love magic makes the world go around—I even wrote a book about it.

When it comes to spellwork, however, doing any kind of love spell can be problematic. Performing workings for love isn't like you see in the popular media. Most often it is best to concentrate on the love you have for yourself and attracting the right partners and friends to you. It isn't about changing or interfering with someone's will; rather, it's about aligning yourself with loving forces around you.

Individuals must be ethically responsible and focus primarily on opening up to the best love situation possible for them. Fixating on changing a specific person will most likely have negative consequences.

Dream Lover Spell Oil: Use this spell when you are single or unattached. It will help you see a vision of your future partner in your dreamspace.

INGREDIENTS:

¼ ounce sweet almond oil

Small glass bottle

3 drops thyme oil

3 drops sandalwood oil

3 apple seeds

Gather all ingredients together on your working altar or shrine. Place the sweet almond oil into the bottle, add the thyme and sandalwood oil, and then add the apple seeds. Cover the bottle, then gently toss it into the air and catch it. This will magically and symbolically send it into the realm of the invisible and bless it. Next, do a small test to make sure your skin does not react badly to the oils. When you are ready to continue, place a small amount of the oil on your wrists, the soles of your feet, and the back of your neck just before you are ready for bed. Be sure to place paper and a pen near the bed so you can record your dreams as soon as you wake. Depending on how easily you are able to connect in the dreamspace, you may need to repeat this spell two or three times until you receive a clear vision.

Love Gris-Gris: A gris-gris bag (pronounced *gree-gree*) is similar to a medicine or mojo bag. It can be carried in your pocket or elsewhere on your body to help bring about positive change. For best results, carry it daily until you feel that it has done its job.

INGREDIENTS:

 1 teaspoon dried red rose petals

 3 drops jasmine oil

 3 drops ylang-ylang oil

 Small glass or ceramic bowl

 Spoon for mixing

 1 red bag made of natural fabric

 1 small rose quartz crystal

Gather all ingredients together on your working altar or shrine. Place the rose petals and oils into the bowl. Stir clockwise until everything is mixed together well. Put the mixture into the bag and add the rose quartz crystal. Rub the bag quickly back and forth in your hands to charge it with your energy. Now the bag is ready to place in your pocket and help attract love to you.

Love Baths

Baths are a popular form of love magic that anyone can do. Taking a love bath means you will be able to immerse yourself in the herbs, oils, waters, and other bits of magic that will help you manifest your desires. Remember the ethical concerns when engaging in this type of magic. Please direct your focus towards the highest good for all parties involved. This way you will be sure of the best outcome, however that may unfold.

Thyme for Love Bath: This bath is best used before a night of passion. It will help manifest your deepest desires and also strengthen your relationship with your partner or partners. It will help improve the atmosphere and set the stage for a loving connection.

INGREDIENTS:

2 cups spring water

2 cups tap water

Large saucepan

½ cup dried thyme leaves

½ cup dried rose petals

½ cup dried passionflower blossoms

Cheesecloth

Large glass bottle or jar

Gather all ingredients together. Heat the waters over medium heat on the stove. When it begins to simmer, remove the water from the heat and add the thyme, rose, and passionflower. Let stand for 1 hour or until the mixture cools. Strain the mixture through the cheesecloth and pour into the glass bottle or jar. Remember to cover the jar or bottle after it has been filled. You may use the bath right away or save for up to 7 days, when it should be discarded.

Oshún Bath: Baths are frequently taken for this popular orisha in African traditional religions. She is honored in La Regla Lucumi and also in Ifá under the name Osun and in Candomble as Oxum. Oshún's connection to love and wealth makes her a favored orisha for many to turn to when they have times of difficulty in these areas. My best advice when working with orishas is always to follow traditional routes and obtain guidance from a qualified teacher. That said, this bath can be taken to help align your own personal energy with that of the orisha Oshún.

INGREDIENTS:

½ cup rose water

½ cup Florida water

½ cup river water

Glass bottle or jar

5 drops cinnamon oil

5 drops nutmeg oil

5 drops amber oil

5 drops orange oil

5 drops ylang-ylang oil

Assemble all your ingredients together on your working altar or shrine. Pour the waters into the jar, then add the oils. Place the top on the bottle or jar. Charge the mixture by playing ritual music or chants for Oshún or with a blessing of your own choosing. Now the mixture is ready to use in your bath. Use within 5 days.

Delightful Dixie Love Bath: This popular Hoodoo formula has many different variations. It is almost as if the hot weather down south, or in Dixieland as they call it, is steamier, sweeter, and slower, just like everything else there. The mixture uses common plants found in the Southern USA to give you a dreamy, romantic love connection. Remember to focus on bringing the best possible love match into your life; do not focus on a specific person.

INGREDIENTS:

1 cup spring water

Earthenware or ceramic saucepan

3 tablespoons dried hibiscus flowers

Cheesecloth for straining

Glass bottle or jar

6 drops gardenia oil

6 drops jasmine oil

6 drops magnolia oil

6 drops honeysuckle oil

Heat the water in your saucepan. Bring the mixture to a simmer and then add the hibiscus flowers. Remove from heat and let cool completely. Next, strain the mixture through the cheesecloth and pour into your glass bottle or jar. Now you are going to add the gardenia, jasmine, magnolia, and honey-suckle oils one at a time, shaking well after each addition. In order to charge this mixture, you will need to bury it overnight. You can do this in your yard, if you have one; otherwise, take a large flowerpot or bucket, place your mixture in the bottom, and cover with dirt. After it has been buried for 12–24 hours, uncover it, clean off the bottle or jar, and it is now ready for use. Be sure to use the mixture within 5 days. Whatever you don't use can be poured out onto the earth, preferably at the base of a large tree.

Powerful Passion Bath: No matter what stage a romantic relationship is at, keeping it full of passion and sensual energy is vital for its ultimate success. It allows for connection on a deep physical level, and this formula will help those times be as passionate as possible. Take this bath as often as you desire, and you will be amazed at the results.

INGREDIENTS:

Small piece of rose quartz

Glass bottle or jar

1 cup rose water

1 cup spring water

6 drops ylang-ylang oil

6 drops patchouli oil

6 drops tuberose oil

6 drops amber oil

3 drops cinnamon oil

Assemble all the ingredients together on your ritual altar or shrine. Place the rose quartz into your bottle or jar. Add the waters and then the ylang-ylang, patchouli, tuberose, amber, and cinnamon oils. Place the top on your bottle or jar and shake vigorously. Then leave it overnight on your altar or shrine. If you have a space dedicated to the element or spirits of water, this would be a good place to leave it. After it has sat on the altar or shrine for the night, it is then ready to use. Use the mixture within 3 days and discard it if it becomes unpleasant before that.

Lovely Inside and Out Bath: The ingredients in this bath are designed to help with one of the most important kinds of love, namely self-love. It may sound like a cliché, but all love has at its core a foundation of self-love. If you don't truly know how to love, honor, and celebrate your own self, your interactions with others will be that much more difficult. This bath will help you celebrate your own divine self while at the same time removing negativity and self-doubt from your thoughts and surroundings.

INGREDIENTS:

1 cup spring water

Large glass jar

1 small amethyst crystal

6 drops bergamot oil

6 drops jasmine oil

6 drops frankincense oil

Gather all ingredients together on your ritual altar or shrine. Pour the water into the jar, then add the crystal and the bergamot, jasmine, and frankincense oils. Shake until the mixture is combined, then leave it overnight on your altar or shrine. After it has sat on the altar or shrine for the night, it is then ready to use. Use the entire mixture in your next bath. For best results, use within 3 days, while the energy of the mixture is still potent. While you are in the tub, focus on being grateful for all the things you have. Meditate on the joys that you have, while at the same time allowing all your extraneous concerns and stresses to wash down the drain. When you are done, take the amethyst crystal and bury it at a crossroads or anyplace where two or more roads meet.

Love Floor Washes

Creating floor washes for love, joy, and friendship in my home is one of my most favorite things. The world can hang weary on us these days, and by using these floor washes I can make sure my home is a pleasing place to be for all who enter.

Basic Love Floor Wash

INGREDIENTS:

1 cup rose water

1 cup spring water

Large glass jar

6 drops honeysuckle oil

6 drops gardenia oil

6 drops lotus oil

6 drops chamomile oil

Assemble all ingredients together on your altar or shrine. Pour the waters into the jar, then add the oils. Place the lid on the jar and shake well to combine. Throw the jar gently into the air and catch it; this will allow the mixture to jump into the world of the divine. Now the mixture is ready to use. Add it all to a bucket of warm tap water and thoroughly wash your space.

Love My Happy Home Floor Wash: Use this formula as often as necessary. It helps you to leave your troubles on the doorstep and make sure your house radiates as a space of joy.

INGREDIENTS:

6 drops frangipani oil

6 drops amber oil

6 drops myrrh oil

2 cups spring water

1 cup rainwater

1 cup rose water

Large glass bottle or jar

Assemble all the ingredients together. Add the oils and the waters to the bottle or jar. Close and shake vigorously. Inhale deeply and exhale your breath out onto the jar to charge and bless it with your energy. It is now ready for use. Use liberally, and discard any unused mixture after 7 days.

Romantic Rose Floor Wash: This mixture is best created during the waxing moon. A few days before the full moon would be ideal, as it will capitalize on the powerful energy of this time and provide a delightfully romantic atmosphere.

INGREDIENTS:

1 cup rose water

1 cup spring water

1 cup Florida water

Glass bottle or jar

6 drops rose oil

6 drops tuberose oil

6 drops gardenia oil

Assemble all ingredients together on your working altar or shrine. Pour the waters into your jar or bottle, then add the oils. Close the bottle or jar and shake well while you focus on bringing romance and love into your life. Next you are going to leave the mixture either outside or on a windowsill where the moon's rays will touch it overnight. Now you can use it as a floor wash. Discard any unused mixture after 7 days.

Hot Nights Hoodoo Floor Wash: This wash is best used in the bedroom, specifically under your bed. It will invoke an atmosphere of passionate love.

INGREDIENTS:

1 cup tap water

1 gallon spring water, divided

Ceramic or glass saucepan

1 tablespoon dried patchouli

1 tablespoon dried hibiscus flowers

13 juniper berries

Natural cloth bag

3 drops ylang-ylang oil

3 drops ginger oil

Clean bucket

Gather all the ingredients together. Add 1 cup tap water along with 1 cup of the spring water to the saucepan and warm on the stove over low heat. As that is warming up, put the dried patchouli, hibiscus flowers, and juniper berries into the bag. Add the bag to the water and simmer for 10 minutes. Remove from heat. Let the mixture cool completely. When it has cooled, add the ylang-ylang and ginger oils. Next pour the remaining spring water into a bucket. Remove the bag from the other water, discard the herbs under a large tree or in your compost pile, and add the remaining water to the bucket. Now you can use it as a floor wash, paying special attention to the area under your bed. If you have carpet under the bed, place the mixture in a spray bottle and spray lightly.

Compassion Spells

Compassion, while necessary, is rarely talked about these days. Individuals can get caught up in the day-to-day trials and tribulations of their own lives and forget to recognize the difficulties others may be having.

Speak Sweetly Spell Honey: The following spell is one of my favorites. It helps you have compassion for others and speak kindly to them. One thing that makes this spell unusual is that it is also meant to be eaten.

> INGREDIENTS:
> 1 teaspoon orange blossom honey
> Pinch of dried lavendar
> Small glass or ceramic bowl

Combine all ingredients together in the bowl. Mix well, stirring clockwise. Stick your finger in the mixture and place a small amount on your tongue whenever you need to speak words of compassion and kindness.

Mirror Mirror Compassion Spellworking: The most important person to treat with compassion and kindness is yourself. This magical working is designed to help you be gentle, compassionate, and accepting of yourself.

INGREDIENTS:

A mirror that is large enough to see your face

1 white tealight candle

1 drop jasmine oil

1 drop lemon oil

1 candleholder

1 small piece of turquoise

Assemble all ingredients on your working altar or shrine. Position the mirror so that you are able to see your face. Place the oils on the tealight. Put the tealight in the candleholder. Light the tealight. Now hold the turquoise in your hand; as you look in the mirror, say the following:

I give myself the gift of compassion and peace.
Fear will vanish; negative thoughts will cease.
I will bask in the calm of joyful bliss
And be kind to myself; I will do this.

Repeat the words three times. Extinguish the candle and dispose of it in the trash. You may now place the turquoise in your pocket or underneath your pillow overnight. After you have done this, bury the crystal in the earth.

Memory Spells

In many ways, memory is like the element of water. Memory can be mysterious and elusive, and it will always transform itself in response to the vessel that is holding it. One of the more challenging things about being human is that the older one gets, the more memory can become an issue. The following spells will help you improve your memory skills.

Strong Memory Gris-Gris Bag: This gris-gris or mojo bag is crafted to help you remember things under the most difficult circumstances.

INGREDIENTS:

Glass or ceramic bowl

1 teaspoon rosemary, dried

1 teaspoon five finger grass, dried

1 whole bay leaf, dried

1 small piece of your hair (you can cut off a lock or use some from your brush or comb)

Spoon for mixing

Small blue bag made of natural cloth

1 small azurite crystal

Gather all the ingredients together on your working altar or shrine. Place the bowl in the center of your space and add the herbs and your hair. Mix together well with the spoon, stirring in a clockwise direction, then place the mixture into the bag. Add the azurite crystal. Next, leave the bag outdoors or on a windowsill where it can be blessed by the rays of the sun and moon for 24 hours. It is then ready for use. Carry it in your pocket as often as possible to help achieve your memory goals.

Pendulum Spell for Finding: When my daughter Nia was little, instead of asking "What are you looking for?" she would ask "What are you finding?" Ultimately, what you are finding is what counts. This spell will help you charge up a pendulum to assist you with finding lost things.

INGREDIENTS:

> 1 white tealight candle
>
> 1 candleholder
>
> 1 drop myrrh oil
>
> 1 quartz crystal pendulum
>
> 1 tablespoon coffee, ground
>
> 1 tablespoon sage, ground
>
> Small glass or ceramic bowl
>
> Spoon for mixing
>
> 3 coins (pennies work well)

Gather all ingredients together on your working altar or shrine. Place the candle in the center of the table in the candleholder. Put one drop of myrrh oil on the candle. Position the pendulum in the space between you and the candle. Mix the coffee and sage together in the bowl with the spoon. Next take this mixture and use it to make a circle around your pendulum and candle. Light the candle. Place the coins inside the circle. Do your best to clear your mind and focus your energy on the candle while it burns. When it is finished burning, gather up the coins and take them outside. Throw them into the nearest crossroads, or where two roads directly meet. Turn around and don't look back. Next, return to your space and remove your pendulum from the circle. You may now use it to find lost items. Hold it in your dominant hand and pay close attention to the direction it indicates. This will give you guidance in finding whatever it is you are looking for. You can do this directly in your home or over a larger area by using a map.

Healing Spells

Water has long been used to facilitate healing in modern medicine and magic. It is also associated with spiritual healing. The following spells will help improve health and healing in your body and in your home. Please seek professional medical advice when necessary. Remember spells are never a substitute for traditional medicine.

Healing Gumbo Recipe: *Gumbo* is a West African word that actually means "okra." Gumbo is standard fare in New Orleans. This recipe contains traditional healing herbs as well as okra, which is said to grant good health and also protection from negativity.

INGREDIENTS:

½ cup bacon fat

1 cup flour

1 large red onion, chopped fine

1 cup celery, chopped fine

3 cloves garlic, minced

1 large green bell pepper, chopped fine

1 large red bell pepper, chopped fine

1 pound andouille sausage, chopped

6 cups beef stock

6 cups vegetable stock

½ teaspoon salt (more to taste)

½ teaspoon black pepper

1 tablespoon brown sugar

2 tablespoons hot sauce

1 teaspoon smoky paprika

1 teaspoon Creole seasoning

2 tablespoons onion powder

3 small bay leaves, whole

½ teaspoon fresh thyme, pulled from stems

1 tablespoon fresh basil, minced

1 tablespoon fresh parsley, minced

14.5-ounce can stewed tomatoes

6 ounces tomato paste

2 teaspoons gumbo file

2 tablespoons butter

4 cups okra, sliced

2 tablespoons white vinegar

1 pound lump crab meat

2½ pounds uncooked shrimp, peeled and deveined

Begin by preparing the roux. Place the bacon fat in a large saucepan over low heat, and whisk in the flour a little at a time. Continue stirring the mixture for about 15 minutes or until it begins to turn a rich brown color. Don't forget to keep stirring because this mixture can burn easily. Remove from heat, then add the onion, celery, garlic, peppers, and sausage. Return to low heat, and simmer for about 10 minutes or until the vegetables are starting to soften. Remove from stove and set aside.

Next, in a large soup pot, heat beef and vegetable stock over medium heat until boiling. Add the roux in small amounts, stirring continually. Reduce heat to a simmer and add salt, pepper, brown sugar, hot sauce, and the rest of the spices (except the gumbo file), stewed tomatoes, and tomato paste. Cook for 60 minutes, stirring occasionally, then add gumbo file and additional salt and pepper to taste.

Meanwhile, in a separate pan, cook okra in butter for 15 minutes, then drain and add to the simmering soup pot. Next add the vinegar, crab, and shrimp. Finish cooking another 45–60 minutes. Remove whole bay leaves. Serve over hot white rice. Share and enjoy.

Healthy Home Sprinkling Powder: I enjoy making sprinkling powders. They allow you to get a tiny bit of magic into each of the corners of a room or even an entire house. This formula contains three simple ingredients to help create an atmosphere of health and healing.

INGREDIENTS:

1 tablespoon black salt

1 teaspoon cinnamon

1 teaspoon thyme

Glass or ceramic bowl

Spoon for mixing

Combine all ingredients in your bowl. Mix well with the spoon to combine. Now take a small pinch and, moving clockwise, sprinkle it into the corners of your room. Replace this every few weeks or whenever you think it necessary.

Rain and Weather Magic

To be honest, weather magic is one of the most tricky types to perform. It involves interfering with nature's natural defenses, responses, and patterns. There are obviously ethical and practical concerns if you are going to attempt this. Like the old song *Pennies from Heaven* tells us, if we want sunshine, we must have showers. An earthly balance must be maintained. To that end, I have included two different spells here: one for granting rain when necessary and another for temporarily holding it off.

Make It Rain: This working is useful to help lend your energy to bring rain to an area. It is particularly helpful for trying to assist in situations of drought or fire.

INGREDIENTS:

   1 rose of Jericho flower, dried

   Large glass bowl

   1 cup rainwater

   1 cup spring water

   3 drops lavender oil

   3 drops cypress oil

Assemble all the ingredients together on your working altar or shrine. Place the rose of Jericho in the center of the bowl. Visualize water coming into the area you are trying to help as you pour in the waters and the oils. Leave the rose of Jericho in the bowl for three days and nights, adding more spring water if necessary as it evaporates. Then remove the rose of Jericho from the bowl and bury it near a body of water. Turn around and don't look back.

Sun Blocks Crystal Grid Spell: This is a simple crystal grid spell that you can use to keep a location temporarily free from rain or other inclement weather.

INGREDIENTS:

1 teaspoon salt

4 carnelian crystals

Copal incense

Place a pinch of salt in each of the four corners of your space. On top of this salt, place one crystal in each corner. Light the incense and walk counterclockwise through the space, then switch and walk clockwise with the incense one time. If the incense is still burning, place it on a heat-resistant surface in the center of the space and let it burn down. When you are done with the need to keep the weather at bay, remove the crystals and throw them into a moving body of water.

Crossing Over Spell

The journey to the afterlife, and the journeys that occur once you get there, are often characterized in folklore and myths as being under the water. There's a saying that water lifts all boats, and in a way it lifts all souls, too, taking them where they need to go. Water as an element, therefore, that has been associated with crossing over to the spirit realm. Here are some spells and workings to use when facing this time of life.

Crossing Over Oil: Death may very well be the most difficult challenge anyone has to face. Use this oil to provide ease and comfort when someone is in their last stages of life.

INGREDIENTS:

- 3 drops myrrh oil
- 3 drops lime oil
- 3 drops rosemary oil
- 3 drops bergamot oil
- 1 teaspoon sweet almond oil
- Glass bottle

Add all the ingredients together in the glass bottle. Rub the bottle between your hands to charge it, then bury the bottle overnight. It will be ready to use in the morning. It can be used in small amounts to anoint a candle or be placed on a cotton ball near the ailing person.

Ancestral Clarity Working

INGREDIENTS:

- 3 drops myrrh oil
- 3 drops lavendar oil
- 3 drops sandalwood oil
- 2 cups spring water.
- Glass bowl

Combine all ingredients in the bowl. Take a clean cloth and wash down the area under your bed with this mixture. That night, write out a message to your ancestors asking to find what you are looking for. Some examples might be the following: What are the names of my ancestors that are unknown yet important to me? Where will I find the needed information about my ancestors? What do my beloved ancestors wish me to know right now? Place your question under your pillow. Be sure to have a paper and pen nearby. When you wake, write down any names or information that is on your mind. Follow up with what you have discovered.

Protection Baths

Protection magic is one of the most important things anyone can do for themselves and their space. Water is often used in protection magic. The night—and the day, too—is often dark and full of terrors.

High John the Conqueror Bath: *Ipomoea jalapa* is the botanical name of High John the Conqueror root, which stems from Xalapa, Mexico, where it thrives. The root is a relative of the common morning glory found in many home gardens. In Hoodoo and Conjure, this formula is usually used for protection from enemies and danger.

INGREDIENTS:

1 bottle or jar

½ cup spring water

¼ cup holy water

1 small High John root, grated

6 drops vetivert oil

6 drops lime oil

6 drops lemon oil

6 drops bergamot oil

Assemble all your ingredients together on your working altar or shrine. Fill the bottle or jar with the spring water and the holy water. Next add the grated High John root along with the vetivert, lime, lemon, and bergamot oils. Place the lid on the jar or bottle. Shake well, then rub the bottle quickly between your hands to charge it. Now it is ready to use. Shake again and place 2 large tablespoons of the mixture into a full tub (strain the formula through cheesecloth if you are worried about clogging your tub). Repeat the bath every night until all of your mixture is gone.

Four Thieves Protection Bath: The primary ingredient in this bath is Four Thieves Vinegar, also called Vinegar Marseilles. This vinegar has been a primary ingredient in spells for healing and protection for centuries. It was even said to have been used by Cardinal Wolsey in the fifteenth century.[48] It is best to create this formula during the waning moon, whose energy will help remove any unnecessary influences from your environment and protect you.

INGREDIENTS:

1 cup spring water

½ cup apple cider vinegar

Large glass jar

3 drops common sage oil

3 drops lavendar oil

3 drops clove oil

3 drops thyme oil

Assemble all ingredients together on your working altar. Place the spring water and the vinegar into the jar. Next, add the oils. Shake the jar well to combine all the elements. Then loosen the cap and place the mixture outside or on a windowsill to charge it with the rays of the sun and moon. Leave it there

---

48   Cooley, *A Cyclopædia*, 773.

for 24 hours, then bring it back inside and shake it up again. It is now ready for use. For best results, place 2–3 tablespoons into a full bathtub. Repeat as necessary over the next week. Discard any unused mixture after 7 days.

Abundance Wash

There is no substitute for hard work, but sometimes a little boost is needed to make our efforts both successful and profitable. Here is a spell to help out with that.

Money Rice Wash: Money rice is made very often by Hoodoo practitioners to attract money and business. For this recipe, you must first make up a batch of money rice and then use it in your wash recipe.

INGREDIENTS:

½ cup jasmine rice

3 drops green food coloring

1 tablespoon holy water

1 tablespoon cinnamon powder

1 tablespoon iron filings

1 teaspoon gold glitter

Shredded bill (this can be a $10 bill or larger denomination)

Glass jar

Bucket

1 quart spring water

6 drops cypress oil

Paper towels

To make the money rice, collect the rice, food coloring, holy water, cinnamon, iron filings, gold glitter, shredded money, and glass jar together on your working altar or ritual space. Place the holy water and the food coloring into the jar. Shake well. Next, add the rice and stir till combined. Then add the cinnamon, iron filings, glitter, and money. Place the lid on the jar and shake well. Next, spread the rice out on the paper towels and leave it in a sunny window until it is completely dry; this usually takes between 24–48 hours. Now you can take the rice and place it back into the jar for storage.

To make the money rice floor wash, take the bucket and add the spring water. Next add the cypress oil and stir to combine. Now add 3 tablespoons of the money rice. The wash is now ready to use. Be sure to wipe down your cash register if you own a business; otherwise, concentrate on your floors and windows.

There are many different spells available to bring about positive change and transformation in your life. The spells here can be used as a guideline to help you awaken to the possibilities through the element of water.

Chapter 12

HOLIDAYS, RITUALS, AND THE WATER WHEEL OF THE YEAR

Cultures across time have used water in rituals and rites to celebrate the seasons and passages of time. In modern cultures the magical Wheel of the Year has become a guide that represents the shifting of seasons, holidays, and celebrations that have occurred since the beginnings of man- and womankind. Each season and holiday has its own special rites and rituals, as well as its own relationship to the element of water. There are special techniques for gathering, charging, and making ritual waters at each of these times, which will be detailed in this chapter. But first I'll note three other water ritual and holiday traditions, then share a water ritual specifically designed for the sabbat Beltane.

Baptism

One of the earliest spiritual uses for water was baptism. The ancient Aztecs used a type of water baptism to bless newborn babies, while in the Sikh religion there is a baptism ritual called Amrit Sanskar. This is primarily an initiation rite for young people as they are transitioning into adulthood. It signifies a commitment to the religion, and at this time they are given new names. Part of the ceremony is the drinking of sugar water, which represents humility, purity, and sweetness. In the Jewish faith, converts to the religion are given a mikveh, or ritual immersion, which purifies and blesses.

Christianity also has elaborate baptism rites that are designed to rebirth, purify, and protect an individual as they enter the faith. It is said to confer God's grace directly to an individual. In the religion of Haitian Vodou, there is a water blessing called a Lave Tet. This literally translates to "wash head," and after this ceremony is performed, an individual has been welcomed into the tradition and is now recognizable to the lwa, or divine forces. A similar ceremony occurs in La Regla Lucumi, or Santeria; it is called a Rogaciòn.

Songkran Festival

In China, Thailand, and Cambodia, water is the main focus in a festival called Songkran. The word means "to move" in Thai, and the event celebrates the movement of the sun and seasons. A prominent feature of the event is the splashing of water in what at times looks like a giant water fight. Part of the ceremonies involves the ritual washing of statues and apologies to all family members, holy people, and elders who may have been disrespected in the previous year.

The water is said to bless and bestow luck and abundance. Scholar Cheng Qian has traced the custom back to the Hindu river bathing that occurs in India. He says that the splashing is to beg for abundance and success from the deities.[49] The festival takes place in April, when the sun is in Aries.

Saut-d'Eau

Each year between July 14 and 16, thousands of Vodou practitioners make the sacred pilgrimage to the waterfalls called Saut-d'Eau, known in Kreyol as Sodo. Saut-d'Eau is located north of Port-au-Prince, Haiti, and the powerful bathing rituals are truly a sight to behold. On July 16, 1843, and again on the same day in 1881, the Virgin Mary appeared in a palm tree near the falls. From then on, it was known to be a site of miracles.[50] The tree was later removed by a Catholic priest in a useless attempt to squash the belief. Ever since, the site has been the destination of those seeking healing, blessing, and renewal.

Sabbat Waters

Witchcraft has eight sabbats, or holidays, that celebrate the turning of the Wheel of the Year:

- Beltane (May 1) is a time for fertility, new beginnings, and joy.
- Summer Solstice/Litha (June 21) is the longest day of the year, and celebrations of growth and happiness are the focus.
- Lughnasadh/Lammas (on or around August 1) traditionally was a time to celebrate the first harvest,

---

49 Komlosy, "Procession and Water Splashing," 351–73.
50 Davidson and Gitlitz, *Pilgrimage*, 580.

as well as hopes, fears, and the cycle of life—including death.

- Autumn Equinox/Mabon (on or around September 21) is a celebration of the harvest home.

- Samhain (October 31) is a time to honor the ancestors; for some, it marks the beginning of the New Year.

- Yule (December 21) is the shortest day of the year and is seen as a time for growth, rejuvenation, and rebirth.

- Candlemas/Imbolc (February 1 and 2) is a time for cleansings and purification.

- Ostara/Spring Equinox (March 21) is a time for balance and renewal. The day and the night are of equal length on this day.

The element of water holds a special place in each of these celebrations. Here are each of the sabbats and their relationships to water, and how the waters gathered at those particular times can be used in magic and spellwork.

Beltane Water: Beltane is a celebration of the reinvigoration of life and fertility. Rainwater collected during the month of May is said to be charged with the energy of Beltane and bring extra blessings of success, productivity, and joy. The actual day of Beltane is said to be a great time for collecting rainwater and morning dew. It is said that if you wash your face in this water, it will grant you the benefits of health and beauty. Washing your head with this water confers a special blessing of success for the coming year. Beltane is such an energized and exuberant time, and I often do magic to capture that and subsequently use it throughout the coming year.

Litha Water: In many groups Litha is said to be the sabbat associated with the element of water. As with the other waters in this section, this will be imbued with the spirit of the time. Litha, which occurs during the Summer Solstice, is about balance, specifically balance between the elements of water and fire. Blessings involving both water and fire occur at this time. In the New Orleans Voodoo religion, this holiday is connected with St. John's Eve, which occurs right around the same time and is dedicated to ritual water blessings and honoring those who have come before.

Lughnasadh Water: Lughnasadh/Lammas is a cross-quarter sabbat marking the point between the Summer Solstice and the Autumn Equinox. Traditionally, as the name states, this was a festival for honoring the Celtic god Lugh. It was a time for feasting on the first fruits and hosting games. My late friend, author Alexei Kondratiev, told me he used to take part in Lammas water gun and balloon fights here in New York City as part of his celebrations for this sabbat. Some practitioners see Lughnasadh as a time when fire meets water. While the holiday is not water dominated per se, you can find creative ways to incorporate water into your celebrations. The word *lammas* comes from the root word for "bread." It is customary to bake bread during this time, of course using water as an ingredient, which can be shared with your spiritual family and community.

Mabon Water: In many ways Mabon is an underappreciated sabbat. It celebrates the harvest and the balance achieved at this time of year. The cool air and the holidays are coming. Water collected at this time is another kind of harvesting. It is a time for rewards, and this water can be used in your magical spells and formulas to help you finally get the rewards you have been working so hard for.

Samhain Water: Samhain is one of the most powerful times of the year. The psychic veil between this world and the next is thin, and almost anything is possible. The days leading up to and after October 31 are a great time to collect water and also charge it with the energy of the moon and this time of year. Samhain is a special time for honoring the dead and those that have gone before. I find it particularly beneficial at this time to visit cemeteries, both those of my ancestors and those close to home. Gathering water from the faucets there while leaving offerings is always a good idea.

Yule Water: Depending on where you live, Yule is a great time to collect water, maybe even in the form of snow to charge and imbue with the psychic blessings of this time of year. Yule is a celebration of Winter Solstice, the longest night of the year. For witches and Pagans, this is a time to embrace the darkness while rejoicing at the return of the light. It isn't a coincidence that the Christians chose this time to celebrate Christmas and the birth of Christ. Very often they situated their holidays next to traditional ones to help them cash in on the celebration. History has shown us that this has become a time for unity, family, and feasting.

Imbolc Water: A cross-quarter sabbat for celebrating and being grateful for the hearth and home. Imbolc is considered a sacred time for the goddess Brighid. Water gathered at this time can be used in spells and rituals for healing and clarity.

Ostara Water: Ostara is traditionally celebrated during the Spring Equinox, which occurs around March 20–21 in the Northern Hemisphere. In this part of the world, this is a time of awakening; it is also a time of balance, when the day and night are of equal length. In Germany there is a custom of collecting Osterwasser, or Easter Water, on this day. Traditionally the water was to be collected very early in the morning before the sun has risen. It was usually an unmarried woman or maiden who was sent to do the collecting. She was not to speak or interact with anyone on the way to the well or stream. If she did, the blessing would be tainted. If she managed to complete the gathering and then sprinkle the water over her lover, it is said that marriage would soon follow. Additionally, the water is said to contain special energies for healing. It was given to children and animals to bless and protect them, and it was also supposed to be especially powerful for healing the eyes. Some places also used this time to decorate their wells with flowers and garlands.

Beltane Water Blessing and Renewal Ritual

Beltane is a time for beginnings and renewal. This ritual will help bless and charge a space and the people in it. The ritual can be done in conjunction with a traditional maypole or by itself. It is best performed with five or more people. You will need someone to represent each of the elements, and also someone to lead the ritual.

ITEMS:

Blue natural fabric cloth

Large glass bowl

Large blue kyanite or azurite crystal

1 blue votive candle

4 blue tealight candles

Glass candleholders

Matches or lighter

Florida water

Spring water

Rainwater

Holy water

Jasmine incense

White flowers (mums or daises are best)

Seashells

Place the cloth on a small table or on the ground in the center of your ritual space. Place the bowl in the center of the cloth. In front of the bowl place your crystal. In back of the bowl place your blue votive candle in a holder. Place one tealight in a holder in the north, east, south, and west quarter. Place the matches or lighter on the table as well.

The ritual is now set to begin. Have the participants circle up. Give each of them a seashell. Begin the ritual by playing an ocean drum, a rain stick, or singing a water chant of your own choosing. The leader of the ritual lights the incense and says the following words:

*Water composes most of our bodies and most of our
planet. It heals, blesses, nourishes, sustains, and renews.
Water always seeks its level and conforms to its chosen
shape. While we carry out this ritual, I want everyone to
focus on the power of water in their own lives. With the
newness and bounty of the time upon us, think about
the challenges ahead and how we will rise above them,
seeking renewed vitality and joy.*

The ritual leader then places the incense on the altar and says
the following refrain, which will be repeated by each quarter:

Water cleanses me.

Water stills me.

Water fills me.

Blessed be.

The person representing the north quarter lights the north
candle, then takes the spring water and adds it to the bowl, saying the refrain.

The person representing the east quarter lights the east candle, then takes the rainwater and adds it to the bowl, saying the refrain.

The person representing the south quarter lights the south
candle, then takes the Florida water and adds it to the bowl,
saying the refrain.

The person representing the west quarter lights the west candle, then takes the holy water and adds it to the bowl, saying
the refrain.

Next, the ritual leader takes the flowers and dips them into the bowl. Walking clockwise, the ritual leader will use the flowers to gently sprinkle the water in the bowl on the feet of the participants in the circle and also on the ground in front of them. The ritual leader and the other participants repeat the refrain.

After the journey through the circle is complete, the ritual leader says,

We were all given a shell at the start of this ritual.
Now, starting in the north, I want everyone to come
forward in silence and place your shell into the
remaining water in the bowl. This is to symbolize the
rebirth and renewal we are experiencing today.

Wait until everyone has completed this. Then the ritual leader says,

After the close of this ritual, we will return these shells
to the water. Do I have a volunteer to take them to the
ocean or lake? (wait for a volunteer) We thank all who
have joined us today, we thank the earth, and, most
importantly, we thank the water. Now, this isn't like
other circles you may have been to. We don't close it; we
leave it open so we can continue to carry the blessings
and bounty of this experience that we have all shared.
Blessed be.

The participants will now gather up the materials and pour the rest of the water out onto the earth. If this is part of a maypole ceremony, pour it out near the base of the maypole. Put the candles out and leave the flowers somewhere on the ground where they can decompose naturally.

Water doesn't just take a prominent place in our everyday life; it takes center stage in many of the sacred festivals and holidays throughout the year. In China and Thailand there is the water festival, where sacred splashing and blessings are all part of the fun. In the middle of July in Haiti, thousands travel to the site of a sacred waterfall and a site of blessing that has been revered for over 150 years. Then there is the Celtic Wheel of the Year, when each holiday has its own special water and rites that celebrate the sacred turning of the seasons.

CONCLUSION

The cure for anything is salt water:
sweat, tears, or the sea.

—Isak Dinesan[51]

While water may not actually cure everything, it certainly does provide solutions and solace for so many things. I find the above quote by Karen Christence Dinesen, Baroness Blixen-Finecke, aka Isak Dinesan, to be truly inspiring. Despite living near lakes, rivers, streams, and oceans my whole life, during the writing and research for this water book I learned quite a lot. *Water Magic* has helped me see and experience water in many different ways, and I hope it has done the same for you. Water has reminded me that there can be tears of joy as well as tears of sorrow. There are baths to get the funk off and also to bring the fabulous in. The possibilities are limitless because the character of water is limitless.

Water is all around us. It is in our bodies and our environment to help us survive and thrive in every way. Getting in touch with sacred water in all its marvelous forms is one of the most spiritual things you can do. This book has provided a comprehensive look at water in all its manifestations, both large and small.

---

51   Dinesen, *Seven Gothic Tales*, 39.

You can explore water directly through the sacred sites chronicled here—Niagara Falls, the Osun River, Nanny's Cauldron, and many more. These sites take on the character of the place and also of the magical people who worship there. If you are fortunate enough, you will be able to experience these sites near and far. However, even if that isn't possible right now, you will know that sacred water is as close as your own faucet. Feel it as you wash your hands or fill the tub and sink in its delightfulness. While the human body is around 60 percent water, our brains and our hearts are over 70 percent. Water isn't just around us; it is *inside* us, on the most basic levels.

Water as an element is representative of your emotions, your hopes, your true vision. It occupies the space between inspiration and transformation like no other element does. We can use this energy to go with the flow and seek our own level of divine destiny. There may be rising tides in your future, but with the herbs, crystals, spells, and ritual advice here, you will be able to navigate all of them smoothly.

I hope this book also inspires you to do what you can to help with efforts for water preservation and conservation. So many of the world's waters are being polluted and disgraced, and part of recognizing their magic is realizing that they are in trouble, too, and need our help.

Wishing you the best watery blessings!

*Take almost any path you please, and ten
to one it carries you down in a dale, and
leaves you there by a pool in the stream.
There is magic in it. Let the most absent-
minded of men be plunged in his deepest
reveries—stand that man on his legs, set
his feet a-going, and he will infallibly lead
you to water...Yes, as every one knows,
meditation and water are wedded for ever.*

HERMAN MELVILLE, *MOBY DICK*

ACKNOWLEDGMENTS

MANY THANKS AND much love to Priestess Miriam Chamani, Gros Mambo Bonnie Devlin, Ochun Olukari Al'aye, Ogbe Di, Nia and Aria Dorsey, Grace Buterbaugh, Alice Licato, Prudy Dorsey, Edith Licato, Alfred Licato, Susan, Christian, Siona, Michele, Vincent, Victoria, Tish, Mel, Dot, Glenn, Mark, Amanda, Christina, Windafire, Tehron, Lex Pelger, Indigo, Emi, Lennora Spicer, Rebeca Spirit, Bruce Baker, Sam and Ezra Visnic, Liam Nadeau, Phoenyx Precil, Scarlett Precil, Riva Nyri Precil, Bellavia, Cayne Miceli, Little Luna, Ben Wisdom, Casey Coren, Jorge Lopez, Phoenix Coffin-Williams, DJ Martin, Phat Man Dee, Miguel Sague, Alyson G. Eggleston, Sue Ely, Mary Cappello, Cleomili Harris, Julio Jean, Jason Mankey, Lisi Tribble, Joy Wedmedyk, Sen Elias, Risa Sharpe, Addison Smith, Louis Martinie, Heather Killen, Arthur Lipp-Bonewits, Jason Winslade, Spencer Adams, Tom Schneider, Freakee Dalton, Damon Bradley, Chris Cary, Mychael Scribner, Kevin Pelrine, Devin Hunter, Devin Person, John Driver, Margot Adler, Frances Denny, Cristina Esteras-Ortiz, Heather Greene, Bruce 'Sunpie' Barnes, Witchdoctor Utu and the Dragon Ritual Drummers, Dr. John (aka Mac Rebennack), and all my honored ancestors. You have loved, supported, and saved me more often than you will ever know; my heart is forever yours.

Appendix

WATER CORRESPONDENCE CHART

Keywords	Love, emotion, memory, feeling
Direction	West
Season	Autumn
Time of Day	Evening
Astrological Signs	Cancer, Scorpio, Pisces
Planets	Moon, Venus, Neptune, Pluto
Tarot	The Suit of Cups, Death, Temperance, The Star, The Moon, Judgement
Chakra	Sacral, heart
Tools	Chalice, cauldron, cup, bowl
Incense	Rose, gardenia, eucalyptus, jasmine, sage
Elementals	Undines, mermaids
Colors	Blue, silver, violet

Gems	Aquamarine, star sapphire (see chapter 7 for more)
Plants	Water-loving plants, rose, chamomile (see chapter 6 for more)
Trees	Willow, apple, ash, palm, bay, cypress, peach
Natural Objects	Shells, pearl, coral, water, blood
Animals	All water-dwelling animals (see chapter 8 for more)
Deity	Nuit, Oshún, Erzulie, Aphrodite, Isis (see chapter 3 for more)
Sense	Taste
Symbol	Waves and the astrological symbols for Pisces, Scorpio, or Cancer
Rune	Laguz
Archangel	Raphael
Magical Lesson	To dare

BIBLIOGRAPHY

Abimbola, Wande. *Ifa Will Mend Our Broken World*. Roxbury, MA: AIM Books, 1997.

Alexander, Skye. *Find Your Goddess*. Avon, MA: Adams Media, 2018.

Amao, Albert. *Healing Without Medicine*. Wheaton, IL: Quest Books, 2014.

Austern, Linda, and Inna Naroditskaya, eds. *Music of the Sirens*. Bloomington, IN: Indiana University Press, 2006.

Banse, Karl. "Mermaids: Their Biology, Culture, and Demise." *Limnology and Oceanography* 35, no. 1 (1990): 148–53, www.jstor.org/stable/2837348.

Barakat, Robert A. "Wailing Women of Folklore." *The Journal of American Folklore* 82, no. 325 (1969): 270–272.

Bartlett, Sarah. *The Key to Crystals: From Healing to Divination— Advice and Exercises to Unlock Your Mystical Potential*. Beverly, MA: Fair Winds Press, 2015.

Barringer, Judith M. "Europa and the Nereids: Wedding or Funeral?" *American Journal of Archaeology* 95, no. 4 (1991): 657–667.

Bedau, Mark A., and Carol E. Cleland. *The Nature of Life: Classical and Contemporary Perspectives from Philosophy and Science*. Cambridge: Cambridge University Press, 2010.

BIBLIOGRAPHY

Berlin, Andrea M. "The Archaeology of Ritual: The Sanctuary of Pan at Banias/Caesarea Philippi." *Bulletin of the American Schools of Oriental Research*, no. 315 (1999): 27–45.

Bethard, Wayne. *Lotions, Potions, and Deadly Elixirs: Frontier Medicine in America.* Lanham, MD: Taylor Trade Publishers, 2004.

Bierlein, J. F. *Parallel Myths.* New York: Ballantine Wellspring, 2010.

Blavatsky, H. P. *The Secret Doctrine.* London: The Theosophical Society, 1893.

Boffey, Phillip M. "Chessie Back in the Swim Again." *New York Times*, September 4, 1984, https://www.nytimes.com /1984/09/04/us/chessie-back-in-the-swim-again.html.

Bradley, Ian. *Water: A Spiritual History.* London: Bloomsbury Publishing, 2012.

Budge, Sir Ernest Alfred Wallis. *The Book of the Dead: Translation.* London: Kegan Paul, Trench, Trubner & Co. Ltd., 1898.

Burl, A. *The Stone Circles of the British Isles.* London, England: Yale University Press, 1976.

Buxton, Richard. *Imaginary Greece: The Contexts of Mythology.* Cambridge: Cambridge University Press, 1994.

Chamberlain, Gary. "From Holy Water to Holy Waters." *Water Resources IMPACT* 14, no. 2 (2012): 6–9.

Cooley, Arnold James. *A Cyclopædia of Practical Receipts and Collateral Information in the Arts, Manufacturers, and Trades, including Medicine, Pharmacy, and Domestic Economy.* London: John Churchill, 1845.

Davidson, Linda Kay, and David M. Gitlitz. *Pilgrimage: From the Ganges to Graceland—An Encyclopedia.* Santa Barbara, CA: ABC-CLIO, 2002.

Deren, Maya. *Divine Horseman*. London, New York: Thames and Hudson, 1953.

De Veer, Henrietta. "Myth Sequences from the 'Kojiki': A Structural Study." *Japanese Journal of Religious Studies* 3, no. 2/3 (1976): 175–214, www.jstor.org/stable/30233106.

Dinesen, Isak. *Seven Gothic Tales, Introduction by Dorothy Canfield, Short Story: The Deluge at Norderney*. New York: Harrison Smith and Robert Haas, 1934.

Dorsey, Lilith. *The African-American Ritual Cookbook*. Self-published, 1998.

———. *Love Magic: Over 250 Spells and Potions for Getting It, Keeping It, and Making It Last*. Newburyport, MA: Weiser, 2016.

———. *Voodoo and Afro-Caribbean Paganism*. New York: Citadel, 2005.

Douglas, Kenneth. *DNA Nanoscience: From Prebiotic Origins to Emerging Nanotechnology*. Boca Raton, FL: CRC Press, 2017.

Drewal, Henry John. *Mami Wata: Arts for Water Spirits in Africa and Its Diaspora*. Los Angeles: Fowler Museum at UCLA, 2008.

Dunham, Katherine. *Dances of Haiti*. Los Angeles: University of California Center for Afro-American Studies, 1983.

———. *Island Possessed*. Garden City, NY: Doubleday, 1969.

Dušanić, Slobodan. "Plato's Atlantis." *L'Antiquité Classique* 51 (1982): 25–52.

Eason, Cassandra. *Fabulous Creatures, Mythical Monsters, and Animal Power Symbols: A Handbook*. Westport, CT: Greenwood Press, 2007.

BIBLIOGRAPHY

Eiichirô, Ishida. "The 'Kappa' Legend: A Comparative Ethnological Study on the Japanese Water-Spirit 'Kappa' and Its Habit of Trying to Lure Horses into the Water." *Folklore Studies* 9 (1950): i–11.

Eliade, Mircea. *The Sacred and the Profane: The Nature of Religion.* San Diego, CA: Harvest Books, 1968.

Finkel, Irving. *The Ark Before the Flood.* New York: Doubleday, 2014.

Freud, Sigmund. *Interpretation of Dreams.* New York: Macmillian and Company, 1913.

Garry, Jane, and Hasan El-Shamy, eds. *Archetypes and Motifs in Folklore and Literature: A Handbook.* New York: Routledge Press, 2004.

Gifford, Jane. *The Wisdom of Trees.* New York: Sterling, 2006.

Hall, Linda B. "Visions of the Feminine: The Dual Goddesses of Ancient Mexico." *Southwest Review* 63, no. 2 (1978): 133–142.

Henriott-Jauw, K. *Tea & Tasseomancy.* Self-published, 2016.

Hines-Stephens, Sarah. *The Little Mermaid and Other Stories.* Retold from Hans Christian Andersen. New York: Scholastic, 2002.

Jung, C. G. *Dreams.* London: Routledge, 2002.

King, Leonard W. *Enuma Elish: The Seven Tablets of Creation.* New York: Cosimo, 2007, LXXII.

Komlosy, Anouska. "Procession and Water Splashing: Expressions of Locality and Nationality during Dai New Year in Xishuangbanna." *The Journal of the Royal Anthropological Institute* 10, no. 2 (2004): 351–73, www.jstor.org/stable/3804155.

Kramer, Samuel Noah. "Enki and His Inferiority Complex." *Orientalia* 39, no. 1 (1970): 103–110.

Link, Margaret Schevill. "From the Desk of Washington Matthews." *The Journal of American Folklore* 73, no. 290 (1960): 317–325.

Martin, W., J. Baross, and D. Kelley, et al. "Hydrothermal Vents and the Origin of Life." *Nat Rev Microbiol* 6, 805–814 (2008), doi:10.1038/nrmicro1991.

Maxwell-Hyslop, K. R. "The Goddess Nanše: An Attempt to Identify Her Representation." *Iraq* 54 (1992): 79–82, doi:10.2307/4200355.

McDaniel, Lorna. "The Flying Africans: Extent and Strength of the Myth in the Americas." *Nieuwe West-Indische Gids/New West Indian Guide* 64, no. 1/2 (1990): 28–40.

Melville, Herman. *Moby Dick*. New Bedford: Spinner, 2002.

Mickaharic, Draja. *A Century of Spells*. San Francisco: Red Wheel/ Weiser, 1990.

Miller, Tracy G. "Water Sprites and Ancestor Spirits: Reading the Architecture of Jinci." *The Art Bulletin* 86, no. 1 (2004): 6–30.

Mojsov, Bojana. *Osiris: Death and Afterlife of a God*. Hoboken, NJ: Wiley-Blackwell, 2005.

Mortensen, Finn Hauberg. "The Little Mermaid: Icon and Disney-fication." *Scandinavian Studies* 80, no. 4 (2008): 437–54, www .jstor.org/stable/40920822.

Mustard, Wilfred P. "Siren-Mermaid." *Modern Language Notes* 23, no. 1 (1908): 21–24, doi:10.2307/2916861.

Nevadomsky, Joseph, and Norma Rosen. "The Initiation of a Priestess: Performance and Imagery in Olokun Ritual." TDR 32, no. 2 (1988): 186–207.

Newton, Michael. *Hidden Animals: A Field Guide to Batsquatch, Chupacabra, and Other Elusive Creatures*. Santa Barbara: Greenwood Press, 2009.

Nichols, Sallie. *Jung and Tarot*. San Francisco: Red Wheel/Weiser, 1984.

Parker, Hershel. *Herman Melville: 1819–1851*. Baltimore: John Hopkins University Press, 1996.

Pliny the Elder. *The Natural History of Pliny, Volume 5*. London: Henry G. Bohn, 1856.

Regan, Kelly. *Field Guide to Dreams*. Philadelphia, PA: Quirk Books, 2006.

Ruitenbeek, Klaas. "Mazu, the Patroness of Sailors, in Chinese Pictorial Art." *Artibus Asiae* 58, no. 3/4 (1999): 281–329.

Scales, Helen. *Poseidon's Steed: The Story of Seahorses, From Myth to Reality*. New York, NY: Penguin Books, 2009.

Simpson, Alicia C. "4 Things That Can Decrease Your Milk Supply," *Parents*, accessed December 24, 2019, https://www.parents.com/baby/breastfeeding/basics /things-that-can-decrease-milk-supply/.

Stevenson, Robert Louis. *Ballads*. Aukland: The Floating Press, 2009.

St. Teresa of Avila. *The Interior Castle*. New York: Benziger Brothers, 1914.

Soyinka, Wole. *Myth, Literature, and the African World*. Cambridge: Cambridge University Press, 1976.

Stein, Diane. *Pendulums and the Light : Communication with the Goddess*. Berkeley, CA: Crossing Press, 2004.

Tollefson, Kenneth D., and Martin L. Abbott. "From Fish Weir to Waterfall." *American Indian Quarterly* 17, no. 2 (1993): 209–225.

Vajpeyi, Raghavendra. "Varuna Hymns and the Origin of Monarchy." *Proceedings of the Indian History Congress* 33 (1971): 50–57.

Valerio, Valeri. *Kingship and Sacrifice: Ritual and Society in Ancient Hawaii.* Chicago: University of Chicago Press, 1985.

Verner, Gary R. *Sacred Wells: A Study in the History, Meaning, and Mythology of Holy Wells & Waters.* New York: Algora, 2009.

Vickery, Roy. "Lemna Minor and Jenny Greenteeth." *Folklore* 94, no. 2 (1983): 247–50, www.jstor.org/stable/1260499.

Warner, C. D. et al., comp. *The Library of the World's Best Literature. An Anthology in Thirty Volumes.* 1917. https://www.bartleby.com/library/prose/713.html.

Waugh, Arthur. "The Folklore of the Merfolk." *Folklore* 71, no. 2 (1960): 73–84.

Webster, William Frederick, Edward B. (Edward Byles) Cowell, and H. H. (Horace Hayman) Wilson. *Rig-Veda-Sanhitá: A Collection of Ancient Hindu Hymns, Volume 1.* London: N. Trübner and Company, 1866.

Woods, Mecca. *Astrology for Happiness and Success.* Avon, MA: Adams Media, 2018.

INDEX

*In a state of grace, the soul is like a
well of limpid water, from which flow
only streams of clearest crystal.*

St. Teresa of Avila